D1352204

CURE FOR BLINDNESS

# CURE
# FOR BLINDNESS

by

WALTER THORNTON

HODDER AND STOUGHTON

Copyright © 1968 by Walter Thornton

First printed 1968

SBN 340 02886 6

PRINTED IN GREAT BRITAIN FOR HODDER
AND STOUGHTON LIMITED, ST. PAUL'S HOUSE,
WARWICK LANE, LONDON, E.C.4 BY C. TINLING
AND CO. LIMITED, LIVERPOOL, LONDON AND
PRESCOT

To Margaret
who never faltered

# FOREWORD

by SIR THEODORE FOX, M.A., M.D., LL.D,, D.Litt, F.R.C.P.

If I were you, I should leave the Introduction till you have read the rest; and I should not read the Foreword at all. For this is a story; and it begins on p. 15.

It begins when Walter Thornton was changed in a moment from a sighted person into a blind one. If that happened to you or me, what would we do? Our first reactions might be some sort of smile and a decision to make the best of things. But after that . . . ?

Human beings are capable of far greater feats than they suppose. Though taken for granted, the achievements of violinists and jugglers, mathematicians and mountaineers, are often barely believable: and no less miraculous, if one knows the facts, is the performance of the quiet man with the white stick who came into my Underground train yesterday, or of Mr. Thornton taking his classes in life-saving or conducting parties to Holland or Spain.

All such skills come of practice; and this book is one more illustration of Calonne's remark that the difficult can be done at once but the impossible takes a little longer. Even to overcome the early difficulties, a person needs a strength and determination that can develop only slowly and with many reverses. Though Mr. Thornton says little of his setbacks and occasional despair, his story describes the reconquest of lost territory by a long series of victories over his environment and over himself. Other blind people will be helped by hearing how he did it and is still doing it; and the rest of us can learn something of how to help the blind.

But we may learn also, incidentally, how to help ourselves.

Someone once said that the happiest people he knew were those with a grave disability they had overcome. Fortunately, disasters such as blindness are exceptional; but everybody has some disability, even if it is no more than short sight or a short temper, indigestion or indolence, or (commonest of all) a tendency to lose confidence and hope. All these, if one made a corresponding effort, should be at least as "curable" as Walter Thornton's blindness. To be defeated is seldom as inevitable as it looks.

The Thornton Story begins as that of an ordinary man; but he is ordinary no longer. Would he ever have been so remarkable and useful if the bomb on p. 15 had fallen a second earlier or later? Those who read this book will get to know him and will form their own opinions. Also they will remember him long after they lay it down.

# CONTENTS

The photograph of the author which appears as the frontispiece and on the jacket is reproduced by courtesy of the Editor of the *Bournville Works Magazine*.

# INTRODUCTION

## THE CURE

If, when we speak or think of blindness, we mean the inability to perceive through the medium of the eyes, it may well be that a cure, in the commoner sense of the word, will ultimately be found: replacement surgery will provide new eyes, or the scientists will devise some way of connecting a miniaturised television set to the optic nerve, so that in effect sight is restored. The miracles of modern science would almost suggest that any idea conceived can in due course be realised, including such cures for blindness—unless Man destroys himself in a fit of atomic madness before these future miracles can come to pass.

If, on the other hand, we mean by blindness a condition stopping people leading a full life because they are deprived of the sense of sight, it is a condition which very many blind people have shown can be completely cured. These pages make up the personal chronicle of an ordinary individual, whose cure can be gauged by how far he has managed to fill a normal role in society, undertaking the usual responsibilities of the average citizen, and contributing his bit to society as he has received the contribution of others. I have written such an account hoping it may be of use to all those in any way involved in defeating the disability of blindness.

Some regard the complete adjustment to blindness as a kind of rebirth. It is as though they tell themselves: "Except ye be born again, ye can in no wise enter the Kingdom of Heaven"—and treat it as "very heaven" to resume a normal life. Without being an expert on folk-lore or psychology, I suspect that both would endorse this judgment. As I look back on my own experience, extremely limited as it has been, the reactions to being blinded seem presentable in far simpler terms.

There was no doubt that the loss I had sustained was serious and final. It was equally clear that the situation had therefore to be accepted, and that "crying over spilt milk" would not help. Milton had at once summarised the issue, put it in perspective, and supplied a good part of the answer. He had expressed the bitterness of the loss in the words, "That one talent which is death to hide lodged with me useless", and questioned, "Doth God exact day-labour, light denied?" To me his answer was salutary: "They serve Him best who bear His mild yoke . . . They also serve who only stand and wait." First must come complete acceptance. Next must be appreciation that the state of things, shattering though it might seem, was no more than a "*mild* yoke". It could be, in fact, an ennobling experience, an opportunity for special service.

At the time I freely admit, the only thoughts which penetrated were that the situation had to be accepted and might have been far worse; and that many had demonstrated triumphantly, like Milton himself, that its disabling effects could be overcome. The idea of enrichment of experience and attaining a deeper understanding came much later.

The Psalmist had said: "Though I walk through the valley of the shadow of death, I will fear no evil, for Thou art with me." Newly blinded, life seemed very much like a progress through the valley of the shadows, but the Psalmist's assurance was equally real. I could not demonstrate God to my sceptical rationalist friends. I could only say that the "system" of faith worked, and that the whole course of history showed Man's need of support from a power outside himself. The shadows were real, the world was indeed "dark and wide". But God did seem to respond to prayer, and there was an inner strength which rejected the fears, just as those around me supplied reassurance and sustaining kindness.

From the outset my wife displayed a courageous constancy, resilience of spirit, and unshakeable faith in our future, which were at once a tonic and relief. She avoided those gravest disservices to the blind of being over-protective and possessive, and kept to herself the natural fears and anxieties which might have discouraged experiment and progress. Until I was fit enough to take them, she spared me any mention of her own trials, the burden of our affairs, and indeed of any unnecessary matter that might have worried me. As mother, wife, reader and unpaid secretary, she carried her increased load without complaint and without losing any of the gaiety which has always been one of her most endearing qualities. She kept her sense of humour very much alive—and mine: it was a great thing for us to laugh together at some of the embarrassing situations I got into. She exercised her ingenuity in helping to find answers to the little problems of everyday life, and took tremendous pains over choosing my clothes with me, so that my morale was boosted by the favourable comments of friends and acquaintances.

The attitude of others was important, too; such a remarkable amount of friendly interest and kindness was shown me. The support and concern of friends was a continual stimulus: I wanted to justify their confidence that in the end I should "overcome".

While some surmount the effects of blindness without special training, thousands like me have good cause to recognise the immense debt they owe to St. Dunstan's. The spirit of victory over blindness is embodied in the lives of its members. This is a spirit you catch in savouring the comradeship of the St. Dunstan's community life. During training the steps towards the cure become apparent—acceptance, the support of others, attaining perspective, and acquiring the practical skills of everyday living. There is no doubt that you achieve these more readily in the company of your fellow-blind, partly sustained and inspired by their example.

The most vital skill to acquire is that of using the remaining senses to the full: if they are functioning completely and continuously, that is half the battle in conquering the disability of losing one sense.

I felt I simply must be able to get about on my own, because for me this was an essential part of living, was life itself. Some organisations in the United States use mobility training as a fundamental instrument of blind rehabilitation; a blind person with what is called "self-dependent mobility" is well on the way towards a cure. Over here we are only now giving belated attention to training for this; yet the blind members of our community surely have a right to such training. To ensure that they can get it will call for generous provision on a national scale.

Recovering literacy is also a necessary practical step for most, although less indispensable than it used to be owing to modern means of communication.

To preserve his self-esteem, a man needs some form of useful work. Many blind women have shown that running a home is within their capacity and gives them complete fulfilment. Other women do not feel fulfilled without some work outside the home; for them and for the men, suitable training and a sympathetic environment are important. Follow-up and retraining in new fields may be needed before they can be finally and effectively "placed".

Under modern conditions of industrial society it becomes more and more necessary to find leisure activities and a social life which meets the individual's needs. It is almost a truism that you stand more chance of achieving the latter by "looking outwards" and a concern for others.

Speaking of athletics training, an American coach declared: "Pep without purpose is piffle." In seeking the cure for blindness, the secret is the will to win. It can be compounded of many factors: the desire to serve loved ones; inspiring example; religious faith; philosophic acceptance; determination to succeed; ambition to accomplish something; the support of friends and relations; training and encouragement from instructors; effective functioning of the brain and the remaining senses; the force of circumstances or economic necessity. Whatever its origins, this will to win is the vital spark. This is the element which produces the cure.

Spring 1967                                                      W. T.

# CHAPTER I

## BLACK-OUT

Poulain and I looked at each other enquiringly. Perhaps there was a hint of disquiet in the look—maybe even of fear. If so, neither of us wished to show it. The engine sound grew louder. It was just before noon on June 26th, 1944—a bright sunny day. Two days before, I had watched a host of fighter planes speeding over London in the direction of the Normandy beaches, their wings painted black and white on the underside to ensure that our gunners made no mistakes. Was this an outsize vehicle heading in the same direction or was it something menacing us, the latest of the Nazi secret weapons?

Several "buzz bombs" had already fallen on London. I had seen one a day or two before as it plunged on Paddington, a few miles away. The engine had cut out a few moments before the load of explosive dived, spreading death and mutilation. Ah well, if the engine cut out, there'd be time to move. These were the thoughts that surged through my mind. We made to resume our chat about the air-crew training centre from which Poulain had come to spend a few days' leave in London. In a flash the noise swamped everything else. Something hit me. I tried to see what had happened, but blood seemed to have filled my eyes. There was time for a horrible fear to chill my spirit before I fell into the protection of unconsciousness.

There were a few moments of consciousness during the next twelve hours. Men's voices shouting, "There are two more in here." Then I was lying in some sort of motor vehicle, feeling cold, and getting colder. I said so, and somebody pulled a blanket over me. Again I slipped into unconsciousness. Then I was being carried into a building. People were coming out. A girl screamed within a few feet of me. One of the orderlies snapped; "You don't bloody well have to look." Again oblivion, until I was driven to awareness by an acute pain in my left ankle. Somehow I gathered the idea that I was being given a blood transfusion and that, curiously, my C.O., Group Captain Locke, was there. He told me later that I was not expected to live. The critical period was brief. I was twenty-nine and fit, and recovery was rapid; with the success of the blood transfusion progress was steady. Once the lost blood had been replaced, skilled nursing and the new wonder drug, penicillin, did the rest.

In one thing I was indeed fortunate. Mr. Whiting, the surgeon who had carried out the operation of removing my right eye, and stitching up the left, was an honest and brave man. It must have been during the afternoon or evening, a few hours after I had been blinded, that I asked him what he had been doing to me. His reply was colourful and complete. "I've taken out your right eye, because that couldn't have been any damn good to anybody. I've stitched up your left eye, but it will never be more than purely ornamental."

I don't remember how I had phrased my question. I do remember that the reply seemed appropriate. Later on I was to meet men who had been blinded and who had not had the same good fortune as I. Their surgeons had not had the courage to tell them that they would not see again. Often it was left to St. Dunstan's medical officers finally to break the unwelcome news to men who had been left for varying periods in agonised uncertainty, hoping against hope that their sight had not been lost. The first stage in the cure of blindness is acceptance. The longer hope is dangled, the more difficult acceptance becomes. The boon conferred on me was nullified to some extent a week or two later by a well-meaning friend who told me that a surgeon had said my case was similar to Esmond Knight's, and I should later recover some sight.

A telegram had been sent to my wife at our home in Burnley, Lancashire, informing her that I had been involved in an accident and admitted to the Middlesex Hospital, and telling her to come immediately. It took two days for this telegram to arrive, and so it was a tremendous shock to her when, some ten hours after I had been injured, the telephone rang, and a voice said: "This is the matron of the Middlesex Hospital. Why aren't you here?" Margaret, completely taken aback, stammered that she had a baby, and couldn't come. "Then leave your baby with the police," said Matron. "Your husband needs you." "Why, what do you mean?" Margaret asked. "Don't you know?" said Matron. "Your husband is one of several who were injured when a bomb hit Abbey Lodge."

"Is he badly hurt?"

"Yes."

"Will he recover?"

"I don't know."

"I'll come at once," Margaret said.

Although dazed by the shock, her practical mind functioned efficiently. She arranged for the nurse who had assisted at the birth of our daughter to move in and look after Catherine, now nine months old. She got our doctor to give her a sedative, and set off for London. Her sister and brother-in-law came with her. When they reached the Middlesex Hospital, they learned that one of the victims of the Abbey Lodge bomb had died. It was six a.m. There had been many fresh admissions from other flying-bomb incidents, and it was a little time before the administration could relieve their minds. Margaret was brought to my bedside. She tells me that I said, "I'm afraid my eyes have had it." She replied: "It doesn't make the slightest difference, we can go on as before." "If you can take it that way," I said, "we shall be all right. I can think of things that would have been a lot worse. We can still be man and wife." "I've come down with Frank and Edna," she continued. "Nurse is going to look after Catherine, and I'm going to stay here so that I can visit you."

During the night I had listened to bombs going overhead, and had heard the occasional "crump" of an explosion. I wasn't prepared to have my wife risking her life in order to visit me. "Oh no, you're not," I said. "You're going back home." I called for the sister. "Sister, my wife says she is going to stay in London so that she can visit me. Will you tell her that the best thing she can do for me is to go home? And will you see that she goes back straight away." The sister said gently: "I think you'd better go, Mrs. Thornton. It won't help your husband if you stay."

During the days that followed the number of buzz bombs seemed to increase. I had lost faith in my luck and was relieved when at the end of the first week I was moved to the hospital at R.A.F. Halton in

Buckinghamshire, a journey which proved rather trying, as the other patient in the ambulance was a Polish airman who wanted to commit suicide and had to be restrained by the escorting orderly. I was clutching a banana, a precious and rare fruit in those days of besieged Britain; it was given to me by a friend, Lady Forres, who had arrived at the hospital to see me just being loaded into the ambulance. I passed this on to the Pole; it seemed to divert his thoughts, and shortly afterwards he fell asleep. My mind turned to my new condition. There had been no time for black despair before. There had always seemed to be somebody about during my waking moments. But perhaps the surgeon was wrong. Perhaps there was hope. Maybe, when the bandages were removed, I should be able to see from my one remaining eye.

When I arrived at Halton, I was quickly put into bed, and made comfortable. A kindly V.A.D. cleaned the grime from the nails of my hands, but nobody seemed in any way concerned about the state of my eyes. Apparently everyone tacitly accepted the idea that nothing at all could be done for them. My spirits sank. The hopeful feeling which had begun to well up in me during the journey disappeared. I thought of the last time that I had been at R.A.F. Halton, and of the pleasant Buckinghamshire countryside surrounding it, which I should never see again. My mind went back to the days when the black-out had descended on Europe. For me, it was to be perpetual black-out. Exhausted by the strain of the journey, I fell asleep.

# CHAPTER 2

## HALTON, STOKE MANDEVILLE, THE INSPIRATION OF ST. DUNSTAN'S

When I woke up next morning, the black thoughts of the night before had gone, at any rate for the time being. The occupant of the next bed introduced himself. He told me that he had lost an eye in a bombing raid over Berlin. It struck me as apt, and slightly humorous, that he should be called Nelson. He was cheerful and matter-of-fact, and the normality of his attitude did me a lot of good.

I was sitting up in bed, and suddenly felt a burning sensation down the left side of my face. It got worse. I wondered in alarm what this new development might mean. The sister came over in response to my call, but only laughed when I explained my symptoms. "It's the sun," she said, and in spite of my embarrassment I had to join in the general laughter at the quickest cure that Sister had ever effected.

There was good fellowship in the ward, but no false sympathy. Although my right arm had been damaged and was heavily bandaged, there were as yet no restrictions on my use of it. However, it seemed to be the normal procedure that the nursing staff waited on you, and I was a little taken aback when Nelson said, after a day or two: "You're a lazy blighter, Thornton, getting the nurses to light your cigarettes for you. Why don't you light your own?"

"Yes, of course. Why not indeed?" We discussed one or two possible methods. I opted for holding the cigarette in my mouth with my left hand, while running my thumb along it to the end with the hand that held the lighted match. It worked, and in the quietness I could hear the tobacco sizzle as the match ignited it. This was something I did not remember having noticed before. Without giving it much thought, I registered that there were two items here which could be chalked up on the credit side. I felt the progress should be celebrated by smoking a second cigarette, and had only just finished this when Sister came along and said: "I've a visitor for you."

The visitor introduced himself. It was Air Commodore Frank Whittle, inventor of the jet engine, who was in hospital for observation, having been grossly overworking. We chatted for a time, and then he offered me a cigarette. I accepted it.

"Let me give you a light," he said.

Not noticing that he had struck a match, I replied: "Let me show you my latest party trick fresh from the press." A moment or two later he said, "Ow!" and I realised he had been so intent on watching me that he had forgotten about the match he had struck.

This episode demonstrates one of the impressions which remains most vivid from the early days of my blindness: that of the magnificent kindness produced by my injury. There was something in people which made them respond to disaster whether on the personal or the national scale—even if in "ordinary life" this was less in evidence.

It is certain that people helped tremendously at this time. Margaret and I renewed the pact we had made at the beginning of the war: that whatever happened, we would go on in the belief that things would turn out right. On all sides I was surrounded by kindness, and I was surprised at the number who went to a good deal of trouble to come and visit me.

Margaret came to see me regularly. Her readiness to face the future cheerfully was an immense help in giving me a positive reaction to my changed circumstances. We weighed up our assets and decided that we could still make a success of life. We agreed to present a cheerful face to the world, and help each other in doing so. The difficulties of the railway journey from Burnley to Halton were such that we agreed she should suspend her visits. During my last leave we had taken photographs of each other with our baby daughter. Margaret sent these photographs on to me as soon as they had been printed. Their arrival was one of the difficult moments, and raised in an acute form one of the problems which had been lying below the surface. Was there any substitute for sight in such matters? It was fortunate that the nurse who read the accompanying letter to me, and described the photographs, was able to do so simply and accurately. The photographs had been taken the day before I was blinded, so that the mental pictures were still clear in my mind, and her words evoked lively and enjoyable images.

During my first week at Halton I had been trying to remember the words of Milton's sonnet *On His Blindness*. Nelson wasn't a literary type, and couldn't help. The R.A.F. chaplain who gave me Communion produced an anthology of Milton's poems which had belonged to his brother, killed in the First World War, and which he most kindly presented to me. One of the nurses read the poem to me from the anthology and I found memory had been restored:

When I consider how my light is spent
 Ere half my days, in this dark world and wide,
 And that one Talent which is death to hide,
Lodg'd with me useless, though my Soul more bent
To serve therewith my Maker, and present
 My true account, lest He returning chide:
 "Doth God exact day-labour, light deny'd?"
I fondly ask; But Patience, to prevent
That murmur, soon replies, "God doth not need
 Either man's work or his own gifts. Who best
  Bear his mild yoke, they serve him best; his State
Is Kingly. Thousands at his bidding speed
 And post o'er Land and Ocean without rest:
  They also serve who only stand and wait."

Apart from the fact that I couldn't think of any special talent I had, Milton's words seemed apposite, and I found them a great comfort. I reflected that he had written *Paradise Regained* after *Paradise Lost*.

Soon after this one of my friends made the misleading remark that there was a chance I might get some sight back. I did not pay much attention to it at the time and expressed my disbelief.

Nearly two weeks after I had been blinded, when I was being allowed up a little, I learned that a Dutch airman who had been in our squadron had been admitted to the hospital. I asked to be taken to him, and found the experience of being conducted down steps by somebody unskilled in the art rather a disturbing one. For the first time it really dawned on me what difficulties there would be in moving about. The thought raised with it the gnawing anxiety of what I would do to earn my daily bread. I had been a teacher before the war. I decided that I couldn't teach any more. I pushed the matter out of my mind, and after a few minutes with the Dutchman was glad to be taken back, somewhat strained by the first real steps I had taken since June 26th.

Near the end of my second week at Halton, Sister came along the ward and said: "The Senior M.O.'s coming round." When he reached my bed, he asked: "Well, how are we this morning?" "Fine, sir, thank you." "Good. I think it's time we moved you to Stoke Mandeville: it's a Ministry of Pensions hospital with a St. Dunstan's Unit. You'll be better there. You'll be able to learn to read Braille, and do other things." "Oh," said I, somewhat shattered at the thought of being uprooted from what had become a not unpleasant routine. "Need I move? I've got friends here. I'm getting on nicely. And I don't expect I shall be any good at Braille. I doubt if I shall be able to read with my fingers." "Oh yes," the M.O. repeated, "I think you'll be better there."

Two days later I was transferred to Stoke Mandeville Hospital. It is also in Buckinghamshire, near Aylesbury, the other side of Coombe Hill from Halton. Even in 1944 the hospital was becoming famous as a paraplegic centre. It was a massive bungalow-type arrangement. I remember nothing of the journey there. All I can recall is my surprise that I should be put into a wheeled chair to be conveyed from the lodge to the Officers' Ward. I registered the impression of very long corridors, quite wide, and reckoned that we must be at one end of the building.

There was not much in the single room which was to be my home for the next eight weeks: a chair, bed, wardrobe, and bedside table; but the bed was extremely comfortable.

"Oh yes," said Sister O'Shea, the kindly Irish nurse who was in charge of the ward, "St. Dunstaners have their own Dunlopillo mattresses."

She had hardly said this when a young man knocked at the door, and said: "Mind if I pop in for a second, Sister? Hullo. You the new boy? I'm Harry Devonport, also a St. Dunstaner, but I can see just enough to get about. I'm R.A.F., too. There are a few more blind blokes in this ward, all Army types. The men's ward and the St. D.'s staff are over on the other side. Most of the chaps here are spinal cases or stomachs. Latter are miserable devils. You want to keep away from 'em."

I thought of what the M.O. had said at Halton: "You'll be able to learn Braille, and other things." I was interested in the idea of becoming a literate person again, although afraid my sense of touch might not be any good, and reading with the fingers too difficult.

"What goes on here? What's this Braille business?"

"Oh, nothing much," he said. "You start off with large dots, you know—Braille for the babes. But the first thing that happens will be that Miss Paine, the Matron of St. D.'s, will come and see you and present you with a Braille watch."

"Oh yes," said I, "and what does one do with that?"

"Oh, tells the time, you know. It's got raised dots at each of the hours. Two dots at twelve, three, six, nine. The raised hands are pretty strong. You have to handle them gently, but you can tell the time quite easily."

And so it proved. Next day Miss Paine came to see me. We only talked for a little while, but long enough for her to register as a kind and understanding person who was also a shrewd judge of people. She presented me with the watch. I felt the hands gently. It was nearly half past two. This was one of life's more exciting moments. I felt as if a door in a locked building had suddenly been opened.

The process was carried a stage further by my next two visitors, Padre Nugee and Elizabeth, his wife. The Rev. Andrew Nugee, a St. Dunstaner of the First World War, had the sort of built-in cheerfulness in his voice which immediately made you feel better. One thing which had most certainly happened to me during the past three weeks was that I had become much more sensitive to voices, and how they were used. I felt that my perception of the character coming through them had been increased by the sudden stroke of the removal of my sight. I responded immediately to the warmth and humanity of the Nugees' voices. We even got round to talking about the sort of work I might do in the future. I gently declined the idea that I might consider going into the Church, but was delighted by the way he automatically assumed I would in due course be able to lead a useful life.

The next day I was visited by Sir Ian Fraser (later Lord Fraser of Lonsdale) and Lady Fraser. I remembered as a schoolboy seeing his signature on a letter thanking the school for raising funds for St. Dunstan's in the decade after the end of the First World War—"The Great War", as we had called it. I had read of his work as chairman of St. Dunstan's and as a Member of Parliament.

Lady Fraser stayed in the room only a very short time. But with her too it was long enough for me to register the humanity and warmth of her personality, plus an impression of energy, drive and capableness.

Sir Ian sat on a chair on the right of my bed. He said a little about my being admitted into St. Dunstan's, and the work it did. His voice was calm, kindly and measured. I was surprised at his questions. They had a matter-of-fact quality I had not really bargained for.

"So you've been blinded?"

"Yes."

"Totally?"

"Yes."

"What about your hearing? Is that all right?"

"Oh yes," I said, rather taken aback. It hadn't occurred to me that it could have been otherwise. I now realised it might well have been; and that being deaf as well as blind must be a terrible business.

"Ah, good, good. Any other damage?"

"Well, my chest has been knocked about a bit. My right arm has been badly slashed."

"Oh. Are the muscles all right? Can you use it?"

"Yes. Oh, yes," I said, suddenly made aware of other horrible possibilities that could so easily have been realities. I was so anxious to convince myself as well as him that the damnable situation of having a right arm I couldn't use hadn't happened to me, that I went on: "Just give me your hand, sir." I gripped it as firmly as I could to demonstrate that my right arm really was functional.

"Yes, that's fine."

Then we talked of other things. There was a curious difficulty about my status, because, when I had been commissioned in the Royal Air Force as an Education Officer, it was never made clear that I was, in terms of Air Ministry regulations, being turned back into a civilian. The same did not apply in either the Army or the Navy, and Sir Ian proposed to raise the matter in Parliament. He did so, and the regulations were altered, but not retrospectively.

Although the status question was clearly very important to me, the vivid impression of this conversation which still remains with me is the realisation, which had struck me with stunning force, of how extraordinarily lucky I had been. True, I was described on my record sheet as "totally blind, with multiple injuries"; but none of the injuries were so serious that they would not respond to treatment—except, of course, for the blindness. But think of all the awful things besides blindness that had happened to a great many other people!

I could only feel thankful. It was clear that blindness was a thing you could do something about; and it was not the end of the world. In fact, if Sir Ian Fraser's life was a pattern, it might be a beginning.

One day Major Blake, my surgeon, said: "I'm not very happy about this right arm of yours. The wound isn't pulling together as I'd like it to. You'll have to stop using it, and have it in a sling until it knits. The wound on your chest is doing better, but it will need a pinch graft to help it. While I'm on the job, I'll remove the tear duct from your right eye socket. It might cause trouble later on if I don't." So often doctors and surgeons seem to adopt the attitude of "Why bother to explain? These laymen can't possibly understand." Major Blake made me feel I was being treated like a normal rational person as he went on to explain the reasons for what he proposed to do.

However, the operations meant I should be confined to my bed for a bit; but Sir Ian Fraser told me I should be visited by members of St. Dunstan's staff, to arrange for me to take up any activities that might interest me, and which I could carry out in bed.

The next visitor from St. Dunstan's was the Braille teacher,

George Killinbeck, commonly known as "Killie". We agreed I had better put off starting the Braille lessons, but he said he would call in now and then for a chat. This he did, and I learned a good deal from him. I also absorbed more and more the matter-of-fact acceptance of blindness as a disability to be overcome which I learned to recognise as the hallmark of St. Dunstan's. It was some time before I discovered that Killie had lost an arm as well as being totally blinded in the First War. He was quietly cheerful, and his anecdotes had an amusing twist even though the situation they described might be far from funny at the time.

For instance, he described the measures he adopted in his early days of blindness to avoid being conspicuous: when out with a friend he would walk along, side by side, keeping contact by touching his friend's elbow with his own. On one occasion they were walking along the platform at Victoria station. It was a little crowded, and he became separated from his friend without realising it. He was still maintaining elbow contact. His first intimation that something was wrong was when he found himself off the edge of the platform, and standing on the track. Remembering it, he chuckled. "And there I was, standing on the track, wondering who'd been mucking about with Victoria station."

The best precept is example. I had met my first four St. Dunstaners. From each of them I picked up something of the attitude all four shared: the attitude of accepting blindness as an inescapable fact with inevitable limitations, but one which in the sum total of life made no real difference. Although I had not yet heard the phrase coined by Sir Arthur Pearson, founder of St. Dunstan's, "Victory over Blindness", which he used as the title of his book, I had caught this spirit of St. Dunstan's. There would still be many moments of doubt, even despair. But the inspiration would remain, bringing new confidence that victory was possible in the end.

CHAPTER 3

PICKING UP THE THREADS

The days seemed to pass quite quickly. I suppose I spent a good deal of time sleeping, and there were frequent visitors. On one of their visits two of my R.A.F. friends, Neil Munn and Duncan McAlister, brought with them my personal belongings, including some of the things which had been in my pockets when I was knocked out. I had been wearing a battle-dress at the time, with my cigarette case in my left-hand breast pocket. From the condition of the case it was clear that I should almost certainly have been killed on the spot if I had had it anywhere else. This enhanced the sense of relief and thankfulness I already felt, to have escaped so comparatively lightly.

Margaret came to see me. The difficulties of the wartime journey were immense. We agreed that I should try to find somewhere in the locality where she could come and live, bringing with her the baby daughter of whom I had seen so little. I mentioned this to Marjorie Dixon, librarian of the hospital, who had been one of my regular visitors. She looked at the photograph standing on my bedside table.

"Is this your wife?"

"It is indeed."

"Then she can come and stay with me. I've got several people staying with me already," she went on, "but luckily it's a big house. It's called 'Terrick'."

I was so surprised that for a moment I was lost for words. Two phrases from the New Testament flashed through my mind: "Ask and ye shall receive. Knock and it shall be opened unto you."

When I had recovered, I thanked Marjorie, saying: "I'm sure you will get on famously with Margaret. And I'm sure you'll love little Catherine."

27

"I'm sure I shall," laughed Marjorie. "We've got one baby in the house already."

Marjorie had liked my wife's photograph. She took to her on sight, and a close and warm friendship developed which lasted until Marjorie died. She was a sweet and kindly person, whose character had been ennobled by a good deal of personal suffering.

Miss Bell, the attractive occupational therapist, had done her best to interest me in the leatherwork and other crafts which many of the men found helpful and satisfying. But I was more anxious to regain my literacy, so as soon as I could use my right arm, I set about learning to type and to read and write Braille.

I had already learned the principles of Braille. It is a nicely logical system and therefore quite easy to pick up. It is a system of raised dots, which are felt by the blind reader. The basic unit is a cell of six dots, arranged in two vertical lines of three. For the first ten letters of the alphabet, you use only the top four dots. To form the next ten letters, the bottom dot of the left-hand vertical set is added. You add the remaining dot to these combinations to produce the remaining letters of the alphabet, except the letter "W". The five surplus formations are used to indicate the common words, "and", "for", "of", "the", "with". "W" did not appear in the original Braille letter system, because it is not used in French, and Louis Braille, inventor (around 1830) of the system which bears his name, was a Frenchman. At first you learn to read separate letters, then letters forming words, and so to sentences made up of words with a separate Braille symbol for each letter. Contracted Braille, where one symbol can stand for several letters, represents the final form used for ordinary Braille literature

It was a stroke of good fortune that I had learned to type to escape the boredom of the evenings when I was sent to my first R.A.F. station after training. Although I had not had enough time to learn to touch-type properly, I knew the keyboard and soon found myself able now to type my letters.

It was apparently the rule of the hospital that stout was only supplied to men who were regarded as needing it. My recovery had been steady, and I was taken off the "stout list". When I made enquiries, this was explained to me; the only way I could get back on to the list was by having a relapse or an operation! I decided in favour of the latter. This was where the newly acquired typewriter, provided by St. Dunstan's, came in useful. I did a memo to Major Blake, reference "R.O.F.B. 1" (Removal of Foreign Bodies, first communication), requesting prompt action in the shape of an operation to remove the foreign bodies which were lodged in my person, chiefly in my face. The communication was effective, and an operation was duly arranged. I not only lost some of my foreign bodies; I was restored to the "stout list".

This was progress worthy of notice. In one sense I was a literate person again, and could communicate effectively. In fact, I reflected, I was in an even better position than before—when people had sometimes found my handwriting difficult to read. With a typewriter I ought to be legible to all; and with practice I should surely be able to type faster than when I had my sight. True, a typewritten letter was impersonal, but one might soften this by writing in the name at the beginning and the greeting at the end.

The question of handwriting had been bothering me. I remembered the painful moments in my early schooldays when I was being taught to write, the lessons accompanied by smacks or the threat of them for those who failed to reach the required standard. I had no wish to lose a facility acquired somewhat painfully and tediously, so I was anxious to find devices calculated to help me recover my handwriting skill. There were aids. There was the metal frame in which you could fasten the paper and keep it still. You avoided writing over what you had written by the use of elastic bands stretched across the frame. There was also writing paper with thick raised lines: it struck me that this must be ugly stuff to look at, but the lines did help.

It was easier writing with a pencil than with a pen, but there were some letters you couldn't write in pencil. The problem with a pen was to know which way round the nib was. There seemed to be no other way of telling than by feeling it, and then wiping your finger on something so as not to blotch the paper when keeping a note of your position with the left hand. A visitor suggested a template cut out of plastic, with spaces for the address, greeting, and body of the letter, and this proved useful. Later on I had one of these made to fit my cheque book, so that I could write out my own cheques.

A letter had just reached me from my A.O.C. I had not expected him to take any notice of the incident I had been involved in and I felt his letter called for a reply. I wrote my letter with a friend's help and using the paper with heavy raised lines. It was a real struggle, and I was exhausted when I had finished. I tried to conjure up the outlines of the letters, and to make my pen follow the images. My friend seemed incredibly heavy-handed as he put my hand in position at the start of the lines. I wrote other letters after this, but it was always a big effort; it was some time before it dawned on me that I was making an unnecessary labour of it.

The analogy of shaving suggested itself. During my R.A.F. life I had often had to shave in the dark, and generally managed it satisfactorily, using a safety razor in my right hand and feeling my face with the left; any cuts were due to lack of concentration or else over-confidence. It was an operation performed thousands of times where the subconscious mind, or perhaps "kinaesthetic memory" (memory of muscular movements) seemed to take control. I applied the idea to writing by hand, and stopped trying to visualise each letter as I wrote, simply letting the subconscious take over. It proved most effective, and I felt again that I had regained one of the things I had thought lost.

I was trying to find solutions to other mundane problems—such as eating. "Man cannot live by bread alone", and when I had only one arm in use, my food had been provided in a form I could manage using only a spoon. Having recovered the use of my right arm, I was now expected to use a knife and fork in the normal fashion. I did not find this as hard as it appears to be for many blind people, but there will be more to say about the problem later.

One other significant episode stands out from these early days in Stoke Mandeville Hospital. There was a steady trickle of men returning for further treatment or operations who had spent some time at St. Dunstan's Training Centre at Church Stretton. Because of the activities of the Luftwaffe "hit-and-run" raiders the Training Centre had been moved from its permanent home overlooking the sea at Ovingdean, Brighton, to this quiet Shropshire town. Colin Beaumont-Edmonds, who had won the Military Cross in the Desert Campaign when barely out of his teens, had just come back for further treatment, and called in to see those of us who were not yet allowed up. I heard firm footsteps approaching my door. There was a knock, and I called out, "Come in". Colin entered, introduced himself, and explained that he had been readmitted from Church Stretton—as he was totally blind.

I thought of those firm footsteps coming along the corridor, and how he had found the door without fumbling. I did not comment at the time, but registered that blind people did not all need to tap their way along a wall as I remembered seeing them do—they could walk nice and firmly like Colin. It was indeed one of the first occasions when I realised how St. Dunstaners learn from each other.

I found the talk I had with Colin very encouraging. Among other things we spoke of using ears instead of eyes, and how sound clues could help to give you the lay-out of a room: how sounds coming in from outside could tell you where a window was, the crackling of a fire could point the position of the fire-place, and so on.

Another great morale-booster was Margaret reading me Sir Ian Fraser's book, *Whereas I was Blind*. This contains the story of how Sir Arthur Pearson founded St. Dunstan's, and the early chapters, which I found particularly interesting at that time, are also full of practical hints for coping with everyday situations.

In my single room at Stoke Mandeville I had plenty of opportunity for reflection, nor were the days and nights without their moments of black despair, especially after a short period of unjustified hope. The bandages had been removed from the left side of my head, where I still possessed an eye; and one day I found I got a feeling of light. The words of my Halton visitor came back to me. Maybe this was a sign that the surgeon's reported words would come true, maybe I was recovering some sight.

Among the belongings Neil Munn had returned to me was an electric pocket torch. Choosing a moment when no one was likely to pass and look through the window of my door, I put my head under the bedclothes to shut out the light of day, and switched on the torch in the hope of catching a glimmer. There was no change, no more than this odd greyness, this "feeling" of light, which I learnt later was general among blind people. I also discovered later that the "feeling" depended very much on my physical or mental condition, and that on some days it was a good deal better than others.

The hope that some sight would return was stubborn, however— but was finally killed by Mr. Davenport, one of the surgeons. I asked whether there was any chance I might see again, and he gave me a very positive answer in the negative! Well, the milk had been spilt; there was no point in crying over it. The example of others was clear before me, this blindness was not a hopeless condition. There was no reason why I too should not regain my independence and ability to justify my existence in society. I had caught the spirit of St. Dunstan's, and my resolve was increased by determination to provide adequately for my wife and daughter.

Margaret and ten-month-old Catherine were now living with Marjorie Dixon at Terrick House. Margaret had been amazed to discover that it was full of people. Colonel and Mrs. Marks, Marjorie's uncle and aunt, who had been bombed out of London were there, with others, not relatives, who had lost their homes in the blitz. There was Bob, an officer from Bomber H.Q. nearby, and his wife, and a medical student, Ian Ranger, completing his training at Aylesbury. In addition, Marjorie kept open house for members of the staff and patients from the hospital. Tea was taken at the round table in the entrance hall, with as many as eighteen people, and the infant Catherine raised her voice in consort with the others in a manner which prompted Marjorie to declare that she was destined for an orange box at Hyde Park Corner. In spite of the strains of the war, it was a happy congenial company, and the kindness Margaret felt all round her did much to ease the sense of shock she was still feeling.

She used to borrow a cycle to come out and see me. This raised completely irrational fears in me. Other such forebodings of possible accidents to her continued to worry me for some months, although I think I managed to keep them to myself. They mirrored the un-certainties which existed in my mind about the changed world I lived in and my own capacity to cope with it; also the loss of an equally irrational belief I had held in my personal immunity.

Before she brought Catherine to see me in hospital for the first time, Margaret had gone about wearing a bandage round her head so that the baby would not find my appearance too forbidding. The morning she came with Catherine, there had been unusual comings and goings in the room opposite mine. The staff, although going about their jobs in the usual quiet way, seemed anxious and strained. There was a sense of crisis in the air, although nothing was said. Margaret came into the ward through the side door which was adjacent, but she had hardly entered the room when a nurse came flying in saying: "Get that baby out of here at once!"

We were staggered. The sister had not raised any objections when we mentioned the likelihood of such a visit a day or two before. However, Margaret obeyed instantly. The nurse followed her out, and explained that the man in the room opposite mine was suffering from tetanus. There was great concern that others might be infected. You could sense the fear in the ward, and you could also appreciate the courage with which the nurses did what was required of them. In spite of their efforts the man died. The room was fumigated. The atmosphere of crisis, strain and fear lifted and the next patient who occupied the little room knew nothing of the tense drama which had preceded his entry.

The next time Margaret brought Catherine they were welcome visitors, and the ward reacted pleasurably to the sound of an infant voice.

My recovery was progressing steadily. For some days I had been allowed to take myself to the bathroom and lavatory, and greatly welcomed this new independence. Both were easy to find, and my first venture taught me that it is preferable to use the back of the fingers when running your hand along a wall so as to avoid catching the finger-nails. Then I was told I could get up and dress. Two nurses came in.

"Hullo," I said, "What's the meaning of this captain's escort?"

"Oh, we've come to dress you."

"What!" I said. "You mean, actually to put the clothes on me."

33

"Yes," they said in chorus.

"Really. That might be an amusing experience, but I don't think it's absolutely necessary. I think I've managed to dress without light often enough to be able to cope."

They both made doubting noises.

"Tell you what," I said. "You hand me my things, and I'll bet you I'm dressed inside four minutes."

"If you're doing too well, I can always hide your socks," said one of them.

Honour was satisfied on both sides. I dressed within the agreed time, but was glad of support when standing on one leg to draw on my trousers. Then I was conducted along to the lounge at the end of the corridor, and for the first time met some of the other occupants of the ward.

There was Bill, the Army captain who had lost a leg at Cassino. He was having some trouble with the artificial one and was rather inclined to take it off and leave it lying about. There were also visitors from the Paraplegic Ward, because these were the days when great things were beginning to be done at Stoke Mandeville in the treatment of paraplegics. One of them was Commander Pickup, a fellow Lancastrian, whose name never failed to amuse Marjorie Dixon. He and I became friends, and kept up the friendship until his death some years later.

Those days of August 1944, while the Allied armies were battling in France, were hot and sunny. We had tea out on the terrace outside the lounge. The wasps swarmed, and a sighted Army officer kept taking swipes at them. Howard Simcocks, blinded in the Desert Campaign, and I echoed with feeling the admonition given this officer by John Windsor. "O.K., bud," John said in his Canadian drawl. "Swipe 'em if you must, but for God's sake don't miss 'em."

I was invited to tea at Terrick House. Margaret came out to collect me, and the bus took us the two miles or so through the village, and out to Terrick Corner. Even this short journey proved such a strain that I was glad of the suggestion that I should lie down for a while when we arrived. I was wearing dark glasses, with a bandage over my right eye socket. I bent down to take off my shoes before lying on the bed. As I did so, I caught my glasses on the corner of the walnut end at the foot of the bed. No damage was done, except to my glasses, but the shock was considerable. I learned the lesson that a blind person does not bend forward without first investigating what may be there, and that it is much better for him to bend down by squatting on his haunches.

There was a surprise of another sort on this first visit to Terrick. Ian, the medical student, returned from Aylesbury hospital just before I left. He recognised me at once. He had been one of the students who witnessed the operation on my eyes carried out by Mr. Whiting when I was rushed to the Middlesex Hospital. It was a bit like attending my own post-mortem, but satisfying to hear his tribute to the surgeon's impressive skill.

This was the first of many visits to Terrick. Margaret and I had been married during the first year of the war, and so had not spent more than a few days together at any one time. We felt as though we were really starting our married life, and thought ourselves extremely lucky to be surrounded by such kindness. There seemed to be a universality of kindness in those days. I was amazed at the extent of it and greatly supported by it. The feeling was crystallised in people's voices. Even in the most casual contacts, voices carried something I recognised as a human reaction of concern and interest, a worthy sympathy. My sensitivity then to this element in voices was such that I switched off my hospital radio earphones when the voice coming through struck me as hard, selfish and unfeeling. At this period, too, although I found the cheery, early-morning music programmes a real tonic, for the most part I much preferred talking programmes—as though I were reaching out all the time for human association. It struck me that total deafness must be worse than total blindness.

Through these visits to Terrick House I got used to meeting people, and to being in a fair-sized company, although so far I found it intolerable to be in a large, noisy collection of people. I made one visit to a function in the St. Dunstan's ward at Stoke Mandeville, but the babel of voices was very tiring and I decided this was something I was not yet ready for.

After tea at Terrick one day Colonel Julian Marks said to me: "You always have people leading you about. Why don't you try on your own?"

"Well," I said, "in the house I am scared I might knock something over, and break it, but I suppose I can learn where things are and avoid them. Outside? Why, yes. Why not, indeed?"

"I've got a stick that used to belong to father," said Marjorie. "I'll get it."

She did so, and gave it to me.

We were sitting in the loggia, overlooking the lawn, which had a herbaceous border running all the way along it. I took the stick, and made my way out of the loggia, feeling for the edge of the step down to the path, crossed the path, stepped on to the lawn and walked along it, touching the soil of the herbaceous border from time to time to keep straight.

As I turned to go back to the loggia, I took my bearing from the voices, and walked across the lawn without following the border. "Fine," said Colonel Marks. "I can give you your solo ticket."

From that moment I tried to extend my range. I had a lesson on the geography of the parts of the house which it was useful for me to know, and the objects I must avoid. After tea, while Margaret was attending to baby, I went for walks with Ian. At first he held my arm, but the second time, as we headed up the hill towards Butler's Cross, I said: "Let's see if I can walk by your side, just using the sound of your feet."

We stepped out briskly, and this was a joyful experience. I was wearing shoes with steel-tipped heels, and my steps rang out on the road's surface just as they had done in my sighted days. I felt a sense of elation and freedom regained, and swung my stick with a fresh jauntiness.

I talked about it next day to Vincent Docton. He was a more recent arrival than I—blinded, I think, in Normandy. He was rather sore about the people who were making profit out of the war, and also felt much more keenly than I the loss of the visual pleasures. But he was prepared to agree that freedom of movement and the ability to read printed matter came very high on the list of what had been lost.

We were both struggling to learn Braille with Killie as our instructor, trying to get sense out of the dots felt by the index finger of the right hand. We had, in fact, attained the stage of being put on to reading a simple book for the kiddies. I thought it was quite ridiculous to have tiny-tot reading like "The Story of Mrs. Spider" as the only material available for grown men learning Braille. However, we plodded on, although I nearly threw in my hand when I thought I had got to the equivalent of the "D.T.'s" stage in Braille.

The dot I was trying to read was actually moving. I moved my finger round it again. It did. It moved.

"Killie," I said firmly. "Just you feel this dot here, and see if it moves for you. If it doesn't, I'm finished."

Killie felt the dot, and gave one of his characteristic chuckles.

"You're all right," he reassured me. "It is moving. Somebody must have been feeling at it with his finger-nail, and partly loosened the top. Your senses aren't deceiving you."

The sister had been most impressed to find Vincent reading a Braille book.

"And can you really read that mass of dots, Mr. Docton?"

"Oh yes," Vincent lied.

"Will you read some of it to me?"

"Certainly," Vincent opened the book manfully at the title page, and tried to read the protective dots on the opposite side, which consist simply of the letters "O" and "OW" repeated ad lib. He concealed his inward dismay, summoned his powers of invention, and "read".

"Wonderful, Mr. Docton. And you've been learning such a short time, too."

There was not much humour to be derived from Braille, and we relished the episode. Amusing incidents were much more likely to occur once you started moving around. Tommy Claxton, another recent admission, was not particularly inspired by the ambition of independent mobility. As somebody who had spent long periods at sea, however, he relished a hot bath as one of life's prime pleasures. It was this that impelled him to get himself to the bathroom. Telling the story, he said: "I can see light, so I switched on the light to make myself feel at home. I got the water just right. It was a gorgeous bath, and I really enjoyed it. One thing puzzled me. I kept hearing female titters. It wasn't until I was coming out of the bathroom that I realised I'd forgotten to close the door."

I was moving about our part of the hospital a little more. When it was arranged for me to visit the dentist, I thought it would be a useful experiment to see if I could get there as I would have done in normal circumstances, that is, by asking someone beforehand how to get there. I asked one of the nurses. She seemed to think it was not too difficult.

"Turn right at the end of the ward into the main corridor. Turn right at the end of that, go as far as the hall, and it's on the left."

I could tell I had reached the hall, because the sounds were less enclosed. I stopped somebody who was passing, and he told me how to get to the dental surgery.

The dentist was interested in the subject of blind mobility. "Oh yes," he said. "You chaps work on echo, don't you?" I replied that I wasn't aware of it.

"I believe it's the way the bat operates," he said. "It sends out a noise, gets back an echo, and that tells it if there's anything there."

"I hope you're right," I said. "Sounds like a sort of bat magic to me."

Maybe there was something in what he said. Of course I had been able to distinguish the different nature of the sounds in the hall from those in the corridor. "I reckon I shall have to rely on the walking stick," I went on. "It gives me some protection, and I can follow walls with it."

He came to see me a few days later. He had an idea for helping blind people to get around. It was an instrument susceptible to the reflection of light from a strip painted white. With this, you could follow a line painted on the ground. I was grateful for his interest, but didn't feel it was really worth his pursuing the idea.

Having a baby to look after, it was something of a nuisance for Margaret to come out from Terrick House to collect me. It would be much better for everybody if I could get out there on my own.

I decided to try it, and again consulted the nurse who was so good at clear, simple explanation.

"Yes," she said. "I don't see why not. Go out of the side door near your room. Turn left up the service road, and keep going until you come to the main road. Turn left, and the bus stop is about a hundred yards along."

The matter of finding the bus stop was not quite plain sailing, and I have forgotten what the clue was, perhaps a seat. At any rate, I bashed my way along, and was triumphant when the bus pulled up for me to get on. My triumph was short-lived. I found a seat, and sat down. I learnt another lesson, that it is a good thing to make sure there is no one sitting there before you try to occupy a seat.

The young lady on whose lap I had seated myself was understanding. She said, with a laugh: "Well, if you don't mind, I don't." I laughed to cover my embarrassment at making such an obvious mistake, apologised, and found an empty seat. Apart from this, the journey went according to plan. Margaret, with Catherine in the pram, was waiting for me at Terrick Corner, and we walked to the house, laughing over my discomfiture.

At a cocktail party at Terrick House we met Miss Lamont, the housekeeper at Chequers, the Prime Minister's country house, only a few miles away; there was a connection, as Terrick was the Dower House of Chequers. Mr. Churchill was away at the time in the United States. Miss Lamont, known to her friends as "Monty", asked if we would like to have dinner with her some evening at Chequers. We were, of course, delighted to accept such a privilege. A few evenings later a car collected us, the guard on the gate saluting smartly as we passed through and down the drive leading to the house. My memories of this visit are somewhat blurred. I remember that the quarters occupied by "Monty" were cosy, and that the large L-shaped lounge, which we were shown to, seemed a much less desirable place to relax in. The dinner included corn on the cob, and ice cream with hot chocolate sauce; I never meet these without recalling that memorable visit.

Visitors continued to come and see me at Stoke Mandeville, among them two of the nurses who had looked after me in the

Middlesex Hospital. I felt it was something of an anti-climax for them, because I did not remember them as clearly as they would have liked. I hope, however, that I managed to let them know how much I appreciated the way they had nursed me through a critical period. Another visitor was Crabby, a friend from my N.C.O. days, who came just before being posted to the Middle East.

He had talked little about his family, and I was surprised to learn that his father, an organist at a church on the outskirts of Sheffield, was totally blind. He was evidently extremely competent. A story Crabby told me about him illustrates, however, the need for a blind person to be constantly alert to all the elements of his environment. Crabby's father felt tired one evening, and decided to go to bed early, saying he had an appointment next morning at eleven-thirty. The family retired to bed about eleven, and not long afterwards were surprised to hear father moving about. He had woken up, discovered from his watch that it was just after eleven, and decided he would have to hurry to be in time for his appointment. It was only when he got outside and found the streets deserted that he realised his mistake.

I wondered how he might have avoided making it. If he had had any doubts when he woke as to whether it was morning or night, how could he have known without asking somebody? To have dialled TIM would have made him no wiser, because it has not occurred to the G.P.O. to say whether it is a.m. or p.m. The state of his beard might have helped, but sometimes one's beard seems to need shaving more often than others. In this country you couldn't rely on the temperature or the sun to give you the necessary information. Clearly it was unrealistic to hope for absolute independence, but then even sighted people were dependent on others in all sorts of ways.

It was early September, and I was only in hospital to wait for my final operation. There was considerable pressure on bed space, and it was decided that I might as well go home for a few days. So we arranged that we should all travel home to Burnley together, and I would come back to hospital on my own. Margaret's father came down to help with the journey.

Marjorie escorted us to the station to see us off, and was genuinely upset that we were going. We all felt our lives had been enriched by the close friendship we had formed, and were firmly resolved to keep in touch. Catherine's baby prattle relieved the tension. Marjorie's final act was characteristic. As we were getting into the train, a man pushed in front of us, and took a seat which meant that the family would be divided. In her sweet voice Majorie politely but firmly asked the man to move so that we could all sit together. She had that way with her. He moved with good grace.

For the two or three weeks which followed our departure from Aylesbury station my memory has remained rather hazy. Perhaps it was not really a good thing to leave hospital just then and become a free agent. There was a tendency to attempt too much, leading to a build-up of strain, which no doubt had something to do with the fact that from then on I could rarely sleep for more than a few hours at a time.

Before I was blinded, I had been able to sleep soundly whatever the circumstances. As soon as my head touched the pillow, it was the signal for sleep to overwhelm me—deep and satisfying. If I needed to wake up suddenly, I could do so, and be instantly alert and active. Now I found I could fall asleep quickly still, but woke in the small hours and couldn't get off again. This worried me very much at first, until I made up my mind that the thing to do was to disregard it. I seemed to be capable of carrying on during the day, so why worry? The mistake would be to let this business of not sleeping as I used to do become itself a source of worry. Such a decision, though it didn't do much towards increasing my amount of sleep, at least helped me to "live with" this comparative insomnia, and also, no doubt, to get more rest while lying in bed awake. I learnt later on, incidentally, that many people blinded in adult life do not often achieve a normal period of eight hours' unbroken sleep.

Back home in Burnley, there were complications. We had let, furnished, the house we had rented from the local Council, where we had had our few weeks of married life before I volunteered for the R.A.F. Our tenants had left, and one of the Council officials, who wanted the house for himself, had acquired the tenancy.

Margaret, who had been living with her invalid father, made arrangements for the storing of our furniture. The house was empty, and I walked around it, listening for the echoes the dentist at Stoke Mandeville had talked about. I tried walking towards the wall in the empty rooms, hoping that the echo of my footsteps would give me warning of when to stop before my stick hit the wall. I thought I gained a little success, but was not greatly encouraged. It was some satisfaction to return to a familiar area, where my visual memory was lively and accurate. I took short walks by myself, and appreciated the courage of Margaret and my relations, who agreed to keep away and allow me to see what progress I could achieve.

When I returned to Stoke Mandeville hospital for my final operation, I was put on the train in Manchester, met at Aylesbury, and taken to the hospital. There was some delay before my operation could be carried out, and as I wanted to see my C.O., Group Captain Locke, at R.A.F. Regent's Park, on a personal matter, I decided it was a good opportunity of trying another experiment. Blindness might restrict one's movements, but surely a bit of organisation could get round the problem of this particular journey. I rang Lady Forres, who agreed to meet me at Marylebone Station, and invited me to lunch with her at Overseas House. I booked a taxi to take me to the station at Stoke Mandeville, and to meet me on my return. The arrangements worked beautifully. Lady Forres met me, and after lunch I got a taxi to Winfield House, which was the location of Station H.Q. The Service policeman on the desk in the entrance hall showed no surprise when I walked in, and said the C.O. was expecting me. I found that my memory of the stairs to his office was not so clear as I had thought, but the Adjutant was on his way down, and steered me to the C.O.'s office.

He was delighted to see me, and chaffed me about the language I had used when complaining about the painfulness of the blood-transfusion. He brought me up to date on news of former colleagues, and then we discussed the matter I had gone to see him about.

Then he said: "What about a spot of tea?" I explained that I had promised to look in at the Forces Canteen in Avenue Road which in peace-time was Lady Forres's home. Some of the staff there had been to see me in hospital, and I wanted to return the compliment.

"I've got half an hour to spare," he said. "I'll take you round and then see you on to the train."

The taxi-driver was duly waiting for me at Stoke Mandeville, and I felt the expedition had provided me with useful experience. It never crossed my mind to wonder what I should have done if something had gone wrong with the arrangements.

In due course I had my operation, and was a bit violent coming out of the anaesthetic after it. Probably I had been putting too much of a strain on my nervous system. At any rate, I had never behaved like this the other times I had had operations. The back of my head was sore, and Sister O'Shea informed me that I had cracked it on the head of the bed in my struggles. I still remember a nightmare I had during this stay in hospital. I was on some sort of aerial roundabout at a fair, and the thing was trying to fling me out.

In spite of these minor upsets I was soon up and about again, and anxious to be moving. The Matron of the hospital, who came in each morning to see us, could not understand why anyone should be in such a hurry to leave her very well-conducted hospital, and seemed disappointed, almost as though it reflected on her personally. I pointed out that I had a wife and family, whom I had a duty to maintain; the sooner I left hospital and fitted myself for some sort of work, the sooner I should be able to fulfil this duty. So I returned home once again, to spend a few days there before going on to Church Stretton.

Sir Harold Parkinson, Margaret's godfather, who had taken a great deal of interest in our affairs after my accident, invited us to dinner at his flat in Burnley. His home was at Hornby Castle, in the Lonsdale Division, which was Sir Ian Fraser's constituency, and he had often met Sir Ian.

"What happens at St. Dunstan's?" I asked over dinner.

"Oh, they rehabilitate chaps," he replied. "They teach them how to adjust to blindness, train them to do a job, and fit them to lead a useful life."

I was silent for a bit, wondering what form the training would take. More Braille and typewriting, undoubtedly; some sort of occupational training too, and presumably training in orientation and how to get about without help. This still seemed to me one of the big barriers of blindness, making a man feel his incapacity most keenly, making him feel reduced and dependent. Milton's words about "bearing his mild yoke" came back to me, but this time I couldn't quite go along with the last line of the sonnet: "They also serve who only stand and wait." Surely to bear God's mild yoke one needn't stand and wait. After accepting that blindness was final and irreversible, you could do your utmost to make the maximum use of what was left.

I was lucky, of course. All that had happened to me was that I had lost my sight. Otherwise I was in good physical and mental condition, strengthened by the incalculable blessing of a wife whose loyalty had never wavered, who had accepted the new situation completely and uncomplainingly; and with whom I shared the joy of our darling little daughter. I had the strongest possible incentive for taking my changed life by the coat-tails and shaking it —and by God, I would.

Sir Harold might have guessed what was passing through my mind. "You'll be all right," he said. "You've got plenty of blessings to count. Like Catherine, for instance."

I nodded vigorously.

When we got home, I told Margaret what had been in my thoughts. Once more we renewed our pledge from the beginning of the war and from my first morning of blindness, that whatever happened we would go on believing things would turn out for the best.

# CHAPTER 4

## CHURCH STRETTON

My gazetteer was encouraging on the subject of Church Stretton. It said: "Urban district, pleasure resort, and market town in Shropshire. Situated in beautiful country on the slopes of the Longmynd, 1696 feet. Twelve and three quarter miles S.W. of Shrewsbury. On the London, Midland and Scottish railway. Market day— Thursdays. Population, 1931—1,701 souls."

Margaret read me the names of the little stations as the train rattled along the valley and I turned my unseeing gaze out of the window, conjuring up an image of green fields, and little villages strung along the road. I supposed Margaret would soon be able to see the Longmynd. Somehow I thought it would be on the right-hand side.

There was a small group of people on the platform near the exit. A lady detached herself from the group and came towards us.

"Mr. and Mrs. Thornton? I'm Mrs. Irvine. I look after Battlefield, which is where the officers are. Don't worry about your cases. We'll look after those. Come and meet the Frasers."

My wife had not been there on the two occasions when the Frasers visited me in hospital at Stoke Mandeville, so she had not yet felt the influence of this wonderful partnership. Their greeting was very friendly. Sir Ian slipped his arm round my wife's waist in reassuring fashion as he said, "Now don't worry, my dear. We'll see that everything is all right."

We got into the waiting car, and drove off to Battlefield, and the Frasers went back to the Training Centre. It was a ride of only a minute or two before the car turned left off the road, and swung up a short gravel drive to stop in front of the house.

"Battlefield," I thought. "Odd name for a house. Surely it can't be connected with its present use." The mystery was solved for me a little later on when I learned this was the site of a battle of the Middle Ages.

A short man with a kind face and dignified bearing came into the hall as we entered. "This is Mellor," said Mrs. Irvine. "He's the major-domo, and he will also be looking after you."

"If you'll come this way, sir, I'll show you your room," said Mellor. "I expect you'll be glad to have a wash before lunch."

After lunch Margaret left. She was anxious to get back to the baby, and felt very strongly the pull of dividing claims. We agreed that as soon as possible I should find somewhere where she and baby Catherine could live in Church Stretton.

When it was suggested to me that I should go to Stoke Mandeville because St. Dunstan's had a unit there, I had reacted unfavourably to the idea. It sounded like an institution, and I had no fancy for institution life. As I had got to know the St. Dunstan's organisation, I learned to appreciate the personal nature of the approach; and it would have been hard to imagine anything less institutional than Battlefield. It was a comfortably furnished, pleasant country residence, standing in not very large grounds attractively laid out with trees and shrubs. It was conducted somewhat on the lines of an Officers' Mess. Mellor, assisted by another sterling character called Bradbury, looked after our clothes and kept a kindly eye on things generally. We changed for dinner each night, and paid a small amount so that we could have a glass of sherry in the lounge before the meal. There were about a dozen of us, and for escorts and readers we had two V.A.Ds, Marjorie Pitt-Watson and Ann Purcell, and Cecil Hay, who also taught at the Training Centre.

Mrs. Irvine presided at the table at mealtimes, but directly dinner was over she always led out of the room any ladies present, leaving the men, if not to their port, at least to purely masculine conversation.

Battlefield was a private house, owned by a Manchester solicitor, who came down from time to time to "vet" his property. The other trainees were housed in two hotels, The Longmynd and Deanhurst. These were on the Longmynd side of the valley, and looked eastward across the roughly parallel lines of the High Street, the railway line, the by-pass—converted into an R.A.S.C. Vehicle Maintenance Unit—and Watling Street, to Battlefield and the hills of Raglath, Helmuth, and Caradoc.

The Training Centre consisted of a house as office quarters, an old mill turned into a workshop, and Army huts which housed the Braille room, typing room, music room, craft room, and assembly-hall-cum-café. The centre was about half a mile from Battlefield, between the railway line and the High Street. Instructional sessions took place on five mornings a week and one or two afternoons. Before these sessions, the escorts would gather up their charges and take them to the Training Centre. Wire fences, along which we could run our sticks, were sited round the huts, and along the path through the fields leading to the Longmynd Hotel, to help us find our own way.

This was the big surprise to me. Pleasant though it was to be escorted by a charming female companion, I had not expected such attention, and was amazed that the training schedule contained absolutely nothing on orientation techniques. I agreed my training schedule with the education officer: Braille reading and writing, typewriting, music, and woodwork.

This choice of subjects exemplified the basic pattern of the training, provision of the tools of literacy, practice in a field which served to develop tactile sensitivity and manual dexterity, and an interest which might develop into a valuable leisure-time pursuit. Implicit in all this was the assumption that the ultimate object of the exercise was to fit the man or woman to return to normal society and lead a full life, which would include some form of regular employment.

The employment side was emphasised by the fact that some forms of vocational training were carried on in the Centre. In the workshop Squadron Leader Cheeseman was doing fine work training men in industrial processes, and discovering ways of extending the range of jobs with machines which blind people could safely carry out. Having had little contact with industry, I was tremendously impressed by my one or two visits to this department, and the apparently casual way in which totally blind men seemed to be handling power presses and such devices, although I very quickly decided that such activity was not for me. In "the chippy shop" where my struggles finally produced a cutlery box for home use, men who would do this later as their trade were producing real furniture. Wally Thomas, deaf as well as blind, achieved miracles of production in the upholstery workshop.

Telephone operators were being trained, and Jock Steele, blinded in the First World War, continued the training of physiotherapists, a field in which blind men had displayed their special aptitude in the years between the wars. You heard, too, of men who were being trained to take up gardening, poultry farming and other trades. In this climate of opinion there seemed to be two basic ideas: that when a man left the Training Centre it was to take up some gainful and useful occupation, and that the fields of activity in which blind people could engage were being steadily extended. The ratio of staff to trainees was very high, because in addition to the escorts and readers, staff had to be on a one-to-one basis in subjects such as Braille and typing. The Commandant was Air Commodore George Dacre, easy, informal and friendly, who had a gentleness in his character which in no way interfered with the efficiency of his administration.

In learning Braille, you first of all learned to distinguish the separate letters, and then to read simple stories in which words were written with a separate Braille symbol for each letter. Braille is inevitably a bulky system. A tiny book printed in letterpress which you could carry in a waistcoat pocket would need to be carried around in a packing case if written in Braille. Fully contracted Braille, which is the final stage the reader attains, makes use of conventions varying according to the language the Braille is written in, so as to save as much space as possible. Although the conventions in English are generally obvious and sensible, some of them seem illogical. Miss Dewing, my first Braille teacher, was a gentle and lovable person, but somewhat vague and nervous. She found my questionings about the apparent illogicalities rather difficult to answer.

I asked, for instance: "If dot two represents the sign for the letters 'ea', and if 'f' followed by dot two and the letter 'r' represents the word 'fear', that can easily be confused with 'f' followed by dot five and the letter 'r', which represents the word 'fright'. Wouldn't it be better to write 'f' followed by 'e', followed by the sign which represents the letters 'ar', and so avoid any danger of confusion?"

I was transferred to Miss Ramshawe, who was much more definite and authoritative: "It may strike you as odd at first that the word 'colonel' should be written in Braille as the letters 'col' written separately, followed by a sign of two symbols which represent the word 'one' followed by the separate letter 'l'. Still that's the way it's written, and you've just got to learn it. You get used to it with practice, I assure you."

I had learnt that there are different conventions for British and American Braille. Miss Ramshawe admitted this was unfortunate, and listened sympathetically to my criticisms of the latter. "Yes," I said, "I can understand that it is sometimes useful to have a sign telling you that the letter which follows must be written as a capital in letterpress. But if saving space is so important, I can't see why the Americans have to follow a full-stop at the end of a sentence with three spaces to mark the gap between sentences, and then a dot six as capital sign for the first word in the new sentence." It was a convention I found particularly difficult and frustrating; indeed it put me off reading American Braille for life.

There was an active social life based on the Training Centre. Mid-morning groups met for coffee in the canteen, or at one of the little cafés. The most popular of these was The Orange Tree, scene of a romance between one of the waitresses and David Bell, handless as well as blind, who played the trombone in the Centre's dance band, and who later on, besides being a successful shopkeeper, gained a degree at Glasgow University.

The St. Dunstan's Dance Band was the creation of Claude Bampton, who ran the music department. Before the war Claude had produced, and managed, a dance band consisting entirely of blind musicians, one of whom, George Sheering, later achieved considerable fame as a jazz pianist. Claude was not worried that some of his St. Dunstaner musicians had never before played a musical instrument. He taught them a sequence of chords in the most commonly used keys, and these were adequate to supply the rhythm and backing for the melody provided by a man with more musical know-how. The band provided the music for the weekly dances which were a most popular feature of the Centre's life. Partners were provided by the staff and an influx of local girls.

Ballroom dancing is an ideal activity for the blind, an enjoyable way of getting exercise in a pleasant sociable form. The sense of balance and the muscular controls which it develops, such as those involved in stopping suddenly, reacting quickly to avert a possible collision, are most valuable abilities when walking alone. The social contacts which a blind person often finds it difficult to establish on some festive occasions are made easier by the conventions of the ballroom.

There was, of course, a new technique to be learned, and hazards and embarrassments to be avoided. Before venturing on the floor, you had to listen acutely to the constant sound clues, which would indicate direction, position, and possible hazards. You had to check with your partner that there were no special hazards, such as tables protruding on to the floor, special flower arrangements that stuck well out from the band platform, and so on. Generally the girls asked the men for a dance. For some of the men, however, the role of patient wallflower was something constitutionally alien, and these evolved their own technique of discovering who was present, and getting themselves passed on from one to another. I learned the importance of designating clearly which young lady you were asking for a dance, when the girl to the right of the one I was asking said, "Why, yes, thank you." One of St. Dunstan's best supporters still reminds me of the time I failed to concentrate sufficiently on my line of travel, and deposited her on the lap of the Matron, Miss Paine. On the whole, however, I felt that my disability had not reduced such competence on the ballroom floor as I possessed.

Local groups gave dramatic performances, and artistes, often fulfilling a B.B.C. engagement in Birmingham, gave lunch-time and evening performances. For some of these it was often a tense and trying moment when they first came on to the stage, and found so many young men and women, some with injuries which made them rather painful to look at, gazing up at them, unseeing.

There were visits to the cinema in Shrewsbury, to football matches in Wolverhampton, concerts, visiting speakers, Brains Trusts, and entertainments staged by the trainees and staff.

There was a little chapel at The Longmynd, where Andrew Nugee celebrated Holy Communion every Sunday at 8 a.m. Catholics attended the small church in Sandford Avenue, and there was also a special St. Dunstan's service in the large church which gave the village its special characteristic distinguishing it from the other Strettons—All Stretton and Little Stretton. Staff and trainees provided organ music and choir. Choir practice was on Monday afternoons, also the day on which crumpets usually appeared for tea, so that choir practices were never allowed to be extended!

None of the evening activities seemed to be taking place during my first few days at Battlefield. After dinner on one of those evenings I sat around in the lounge. One or two people were in their rooms. The single chaps had been collected by their "dates". I had declined an invitation to go out to the "local"; perhaps it was nervous strain, but my stomach felt as though it might rebel violently against the invasion of beer. I wandered into the hall, wondering whether to go up to my room to get a Braille book.

Ted Barton came down the stairs. He was also ex-R.A.F., V.R. blinded in India, and had once rowed for Emmanuel College, Cambridge. "Hullo, who's that?" he said in his slow rather stolid voice, which seemed to bely the academic distinction he had achieved at Cambridge.

I announced myself.

Although I had been at Battlefield only a few days, I had already heard that his blindness had hit Ted Barton very hard indeed, and that at first he used to sit around in the house for hours, morose and dejected. Mellor in his quiet way had done a good deal to help Ted through this phase, and to the end of his stay at Battlefield there was a reminder of this each morning, as Mellor went into his room at ten to eight, switched on the radio, and said: "Lift up your heart, Mr. Barton." I had also gathered that Ted was now efficient at getting about on his own, and went about a good deal without escort.

"Oh, hullo," he said. "Feel like going for a walk?"

"Thanks," I said, "I'd like to. I'll just get my stick."

It was the one Marjorie had given me at Terrick.

We went out into the October night air. In the distance a train whistled down the valley. It faded away, and all was calm and still. We stood on the drive for a moment before moving off. Ted listened appreciatively.

"Just the job," he commented. "Come on, I've some lovely echoes I want to show you."

He pointed out that, on the edge of the lawn immediately in front of the house door, a piece of wood had been laid to act as a marker for men coming in on their own and following the lawn round from the gate.

We turned left, and followed the lawn round, touching it with our sticks.

"You want to keep a bit to the left. There's a holly tree just inside on the right as you go out, which is a bit nasty if you walk into it." We turned right down Sandford Avenue. Ted went ahead, touching the hedge on his right to keep on the narrow path. "The first road we cross is Watling Street, and then we come to the by-pass," said my mentor. "I always go round the corner a bit and then cross at right angles to make sure I don't go wandering off into the middle of the road."

We crossed the by-pass. There was no traffic about at all.

"You have to be careful crossing here during the day," said Ted. "You get Army vehicles around from the Maintenance Unit place."

He walked in the road, following the kerb with his stick. I stopped.

"Hey. Isn't this asking for it rather? Wouldn't we be better on the footpath?"

"You please yourself," he replied. "I go on the footpath going over the bridge because it's a bit narrow there, but you don't get lamp-posts and trees and things in the road."

For the moment I accepted his argument.

We came to a break in the kerb.

"That leads into the park," explained Ted. "We might have a look at it one of these days."

We went on past the entrance to the goods yard of the station— "You don't want to get lost down there." We continued past the Training Centre.

Suddenly Ted stoppped. He tapped his stick once or twice. "Just listen to that," he told me. "Isn't that a beautiful echo! There's a lamp-post there."

I checked. Yes, indeed, there was a lamp-post there, but although I listened with every nerve I possessed, I couldn't detect any difference in the sounds.

Ted was obviously disappointed. It was clear he was proud of this particular echo.

"Never mind," he said. "It'll come. I couldn't get it at first."

He had more success when he demonstrated that we were passing an alley-way. The difference in sound was very marked, and I had no difficulty at all in recognising it.

We returned to Battlefield, and he showed me how to tell when we had reached the right entrance. The gate was fastened back, and I ran my hands over it so that I could have a means of checking that I had found the right drive.

I couldn't find the board on the edge of the lawn, which marked the point opposite the door of the house, but could hear Ted going in, and made for the sound.

Mellor came into the hall as we entered. "And where might you two young gentlemen have been?" he asked. "Just been showing him the sights of the town," Ted explained.

"Oh," said Mellor, "I've just been making a cup of tea. I expect you'd like one."

We sat in the lounge, and talked about this and that. Inevitably we came back to the subject of getting about alone. "I felt I simply had to get out," said Ted, "so one evening I just took off. I'd much rather go out at night on my own than in the day. It's quieter, and you can hear things better, and there are fewer people around to bother you."

"I suppose that could have its snags," I suggested. He laughed.

"Yes. There was one occasion when I did get lost. They sent out a search party to look for me. I'd strayed into somebody's garden, and there was a flight of steps going down, so I thought I'd better stay where I was and shout."

"This echo business," I said. "Does it really help?"

"Oh yes. Some blokes are red hot at it. Take Tommy Milligan. First War bloke, teaches Braille shorthand. He walks along a pavement keeping a yard away from the wall just by echo. Carries a stick but doesn't seem to use it much. Says he has it under his arm just for balance. And there's Bob Bridger, who also teaches Braille. He was born blind, and seems uncanny at times. We were walking along the footpath at the Training Centre the other day, and he was telling me as we passed the end of each hut, and you know they're yards away."

"I'm surprised they don't try and teach this stuff," I said.

"Oh, I don't think it's so surprising," he answered. "I reckon our blokes have enough to cope with as it is. It's very much up to the individual to decide whether he wants to bother or not and how much or little he wants to do."

The reply seemed reasonable, and again I accepted it for the time being, although I couldn't help feeling that there seemed aspects of the business that could be taught. In any case there were a lot of very experienced people in the organisation, and it had obviously done a tremendous job with the First War men.

"Ah well, time to turn in. Thanks for the walk. I reckon I should be able to find the Training Centre now."

"Sure. I'll show you where The Plough is some time. Good night."

Ted and I were to make a great many joint expeditions, in various parts of the country, but that was in the unknown future. For the present, as I went up to bed, I felt I had been "launched" in Church Stretton terms. I could get to the Training Centre on my own, but there wouldn't be much point in doing so, since we all left the house together with Marjorie and Ann, our escorts. Coming back was different, since people would finish their lessons at different times, and you had to hang about until all were mustered. So on the way down next morning I said to Marjorie: "If I'm not around at lunch time, don't wait for me. I'll be making my own way back. I've been having a geography lesson from Ted."

"All right," laughed Marjorie. "What time do we send the search party out?"

It wasn't necessary. This time I didn't wander off into the goods yard or the park, or go astray in Watling Street or turn in at the wrong drive; although later on, when I wasn't really thinking about what I was doing, I contrived to make these mistakes at one time or another. I was encouraged. There was no reason why I shouldn't do a good deal more of this. It would no doubt be a long process, and subject always to inevitable limitations, but at least it was on the road towards recovering the independence I had lost.

That was the way it worked out. It was by no means all as plain sailing as that first walk back from the Training Centre. There were times when I had to drive myself to make the effort to walk alone, when the feeling of light before my eyes had gone completely, and all was black and I felt hemmed in by hard things, close at hand, which I was going to crash into at any moment. There was a pretty constant strain attached to walking about alone, with always the risk of an unpleasant collision or some other hazard; but it seemed well worth these risks to be a free agent.

One of the great things about life at Battlefield was the way we learned from each other. The casual acceptance of the hazards struck me as appropriate. At lunch one day, somebody said: "If you go near that garage beyond the High Street, watch out there isn't a car up on the ramp. Caught myself a hell of a crack there this morning"—and went on to talk about something else. Or there was the man who complained with some feeling that his escort had walked him into a lamp-post while she was looking in another direction. He got scant sympathy. "Well, you b.f., you've got a stick. Why don't you protect yourself with it?"

There were highlights in the progress towards independent mobility, but undoubtedly the most significant was the first time my perception of echo variation told me there was an obstacle near. Cecil Hay had found lodgings for Margaret and Catherine in

Watling Street. I had been in to see them, and had passed the Sandford Hotel on my way back to Battlefield when it seemed to me there was something on my left. By now I was using my walking-stick in a manner which I hoped looked natural, swinging it as I would have done in my sighted days, instead of tapping along the wall. I stopped dead, and felt out gingerly with my stick. It touched a pillar-box, a yard or so away: like Archimedes himself I could have cried "Eureka!" Instead I walked up and down past the pillar-box, to make sure that the operation of my newly-acquired "obstacle sense" was no flash in the pan. Each time I got that feeling, so difficult to define, that there was something there.

Research has now proved that the operation of this obstacle sense is through the detection of echoes in the higher sound frequencies, the sound rising as you get near the obstacle. To me at the time it was just a vague feeling, defying definition, but real and helpful. Later, probably because of occasions when it didn't work and I suffered in the collision, the detection of an obstacle through this developed hearing sense seemed to be accompanied by a shadow flitting across the greyness in front of my eyes.

I believe it was Helen Keller who said that "God never closes a door but He opens a window." That seems to me profoundly true, but I do not think it represents a state of automatic compensation without effort on the part of the individual concerned. This struck me very strongly, again in Watling Street, when I was struggling back to Battlefield through thick snow from Margaret's lodgings. I had been told it was foolish to try to do the journey alone under such conditions, when all the usual landmarks were obliterated and guiding echoes were blanketed out. With Cecil Hay's help I had worked out a route which gave me contact with a guide line most of the way. It still meant a big effort, and I nearly jumped out of my skin when a man spoke to me, apparently out of nowhere. "Of course, you blind chaps get an extra sense, don't you?"

I just restrained the temptation to say "You should try it, brother." I was angry with myself for having jumped when he spoke to me so unexpectedly. This is a reaction, incidentally, which I still experience when someone speaks to me and I haven't realised anyone is there.

"I could do with an extra sense in this stuff," I answered, and walked on.

The desire to be able to get about on my own continued to act as a strong motivating force. I had had some rather traumatic experiences on my ventures, but this seemed inevitable, and so had just to be accepted. The apparent inevitability of these episodes in which you suffered shock or injury persuaded me that the St. Dunstan's policy was right—of providing escorts, and leaving it to the individual to develop a technique of independent mobility if he wished. Some men had been under tremendous strain before being blinded. Some had head and other injuries, from which they had not entirely recovered. If getting about alone was bound to be accompanied by stresses and injuries of the sort I was experiencing, it would hardly be sensible to increase this load, however desirable the goal of achievement might appear. Such an effort would impose a drain on resources which might well be better and more fruitfully applied in other directions.

People wanted to be helpful, in fact it seemed to give them quite a lift to have the opportunity of helping; so why not let them? The difficulty was that such people were not always available when you wanted them. There were times, too, when you felt that the help you needed was a strain on goodwill. If you went to the hairdresser's, for example, you had to arrange to be escorted, and the escort either had to wait, or call back later. All right then, leave it to the individual to decide for himself whether he should learn to get about alone, but I had to accept that there would always be situations when help of some kind was necessary; after all I had sometimes needed help even in my sighted days. What I wanted to do was to satisfy myself that I could get about alone enough to make life tolerable.

So I continued my experiments, and was content to know I could reach the places I wanted to in Church Stretton independently if necessary. Unfortunately, some of the sighted staff did not seem to understand my objective—I felt independence was almost a dirty word for them. They made rather querulous comments about my efforts in this direction, instead of appreciating that the wish to retrieve this lost power was part of the fibre of my being, a basic need they should have been trying to help satisfy.

In the black-out in London I had learnt that you could easily turn a corner without knowing you had done so. I now discovered that this matter of angles is one of the fundamental problems in achieving blind mobility. Unless you developed some sort of checking technique, you might well turn through 180 or even 360 degrees without realising it. Ted had warned me of the possibility of straying into the station goods yard when I was near the Training Centre. The possible complications of the angles of the roads in this area was brought home to me one morning when I was walking down to the Centre with Marjorie Pitt-Watson.

I was checking on the position of one or two places as we walked along. "And the Training Centre is over there," I said, pointing. Marjorie laughed. "I'm afraid not. It's there." She moved my arm about forty degrees. "That's impossible," I said. "Impossible or not, it's there," said Marjorie, and proceeded to show me.

When blind people first start to learn to get about alone, they adopt a tapping technique, and invariably make a lot of noise, as though the noise were a reassurance to them. I can still remember the noise I made as I went down the hospital road back to the ward at Stoke Mandeville after my first solo visit to Terrick. My taps were quieter at Church Stretton, but I still needed the assurance of a guide line such as a wall, kerb or hedge, in order to maintain my line of travel and keep aware of my position. I felt this made me unduly conspicuous, and tried to find a more natural way of walking.

When I was not in a congested area, why not use my walking-stick as I would have done in my sighted days? If necessary, I could give it a little flick to the side now and then, to make or keep contact with a wall or other guide line and discover something about my surroundings. I wouldn't have the same degree of protection against obstacles immediately ahead, but on the quiet country road I could walk in the roadway, keeping my ears skinned for the occasional motor vehicle or bicycle. The sense of freedom made the little extra risk seem worth while.

If I thought there might be obstacles in my path, I held the stick so that it projected in front of me, though embarrassed to be walking like this. Of course I had no protection except my guardian angel's against the unexpected drop in level, but this seemed just one of those unavoidable risks. Slowly I learnt to recognise that pavements almost always slope a little towards a kerb's edge, and to protect myself against that jar to the spine when I stepped off a kerb unexpectedly.

Simple attempts to find places, after obtaining advance verbal description of the route, proved successful; and I was greatly encouraged by two longer journeys of about three miles.

The first of these was a night walk to join a group who were having a get-together at The Green Dragon at Little Stretton. As I crossed Watling Street, I thought for a few seconds that I had lost my bearings. Milton's phrase, "this dark world and wide", suddenly came into my mind with great force, and I told myself I was a fool not to have gone earlier with the escorts. Then I heard a lorry on the by-pass, got my bearings, and was reassured. It seemed a long way, and several times I wondered if I had missed my way, but then I found myself on a little lane with a wall on my right, which fitted the description of the area very near my goal. I was jubilant, and moved into the middle of the lane, swinging my stick as I walked. Whether there was a slight turn in the lane, or whether I had altered my line of travel, I do not know, but a very short time later I found my left foot in thin air, and myself standing in the stream which skirted the lane.

Various thoughts flashed through my mind: "Don't halloo till you're out of the wood"; "Serves me right for not being more careful"; "Good thing I didn't fall on my back, or I should be very wet." I scrambled back on to the road, and assessed the damage. My shoes, socks, and the bottom of my trousers were wet, but perhaps nobody would notice. I moved over to the wall, tapped my way along, and soon heard the sounds which told me I was there. All I had to do was find the entrance. Luckily someone came out just then. I went in, and someone else said: "Come this way, your friends are in here."

My sleep that night was somewhat disturbed, but I felt it had been worth it. I had proved my theory to my own satisfaction, and learned some valuable lessons. The chief lesson was that when making a journey along a route you didn't know, it was best to ask about possible special perils.

Perhaps the route was simpler, but the next journey of this kind I made passed off without incident, a complete success. Some people from Battlefield were going for a walk through the fields to Chelmick, to have tea at a splendid café kept by two sisters called Jones. In those days of wartime scarcity, their teas—with delicious cakes as a highlight—were something to make the mouth water.

I asked about the route, and learnt that the journey by road was quite easy, so long as you remembered to turn right at Hope Bowdler and did not overshoot the turning on the right a few hundred yards further on. It was a little further by road, so I set off before the main party, walking up the middle of Sandford Avenue, as there was no traffic. As I dropped down the hill into Hope Bowdler, a solitary car went along the road which formed the T junction. That was considerate of him—there was my turning. I turned right and followed the grass verge. I had to take the next turning to the right, but of course must make sure I didn't mistake somebody's drive for the road. I found what must be the turning, and had this confirmed in a little while when I found the road going uphill. Somebody was working in the field on my right. I called out: "Excuse me—isn't the Misses Jones's place near here?" It was just a little further on, I was told. I found the entrance. One of the Misses Jones was just walking out of the bakehouse to the cottage where the teas were served. There was a delicious smell of baking.

"Good afternoon," she said in her rather thin voice. "I'm not quite ready for you."

I explained that I had walked on ahead, and that the others would be there soon. She found me a seat in the yard outside the cottage, and I rested, well pleased with this second proof that the system was a practicable one.

In hospital at Stoke Mandeville Colin Beaumont-Edmonds had talked to me about Church Stretton, and the sort of place it was.

From him I had gathered some idea of the lay-out of the village and its surroundings. It was a region I did not know at all, and I wondered whether it would be possible for me to get visual images of the place which would be reasonably accurate, to join those other visual memories I retained from my sighted days. I could recall the black bulk of Pendle Hill across the valley from the heights above Burnley; the lush green leafiness of the corner near Shottery; the metallic mass of Blackpool Tower rising from the jumble of the "golden mile"; the beauty of the light on the lake as we emerged from the grottoes of Han; the view over the tree-tops towards the mountains of the Lake District from the gunroom flat at Hornby Castle; the entrance to the harbour at Belle Île off the Breton coast, or the road zigzagging up the Feldberg in the Black Forest. Would I be able to gather such mental images at Church Stretton? Would a word, a scent or a sound evoke pictures to "flash across that inward eye"?

It was an interesting idea, and one realised in part. From the descriptions of my sighted friends, supplemented by the impressions gained during my walks or rides on horseback or tandem, I built up a series of mental images which I believe are fairly accurate. Pictures on a small canvas would spring into clear relief, like the footbridge across the railway line, the Army huts which made up the training centre, the drive to Battlefield, and so on. But I could not conjure up a view which covered a wide landscape. It seemed as though the imagination was there being fed only by my remaining senses, and would not convert into live images what came only from the words of others and my own inferences.

I referred just now to rides on horseback or tandem, but in fact I only went tandem-riding once, although it was a popular activity with some of the men, Lady Buckmaster being the tandemist *par excellence*. On my one ride Anne Purcell occupied the front seat. We rode along the valley as far as Craven Arms, and returned without mishap, although I was firmly convinced that the operation had been in total defiance of normal gravitational forces and that this miracle was unlikely to be repeated.

I found horse riding an exciting new experience. Mounted on Wiseman, who lived up to his name—the tacking manoeuvres to make a steep descent were certainly his idea and not mine—and with Susan Cantey as my instructress, I enjoyed exploring the countryside, and sometimes the thrill of a mad gallop in Ash's valley or on the top of the Longmynd. I decided that if I were thrown, I would hunch up into a ball and try to roll clear, but the idea never needed to be put to the test.

The weeks passed, and the Training Centre broke up for the Christmas holidays. Of all the instructors, I felt that those engaged in teaching Braille must surely be in the greatest need of a break. Although the ability to read and write Braille represented the return to literacy, the speed of reading of even the most competent remained pitifully slow. It is rare for a person blinded in adult life to attain anything approaching the speeds achieved by the congenitally blind, who manage as much as 140 words a minute. We tended to be preoccupied with our own struggles to master those tantalising dots, but occasionally a slight touch of impatience in the instructor's voice would reveal something of the tedium he must have felt as his pupils battled away, striving to substitute the tactile sense for the visual, to establish the Braille shapes as firmly in the mental processes as the printed word. Even today, more than two decades after I was blinded, I find that the printed outline of a word jumps to mind much more readily than its Braille equivalent.

Thoughts of the journeys home prompted stories about trains. We were acutely self-conscious about the attitude of the sighted towards us. There was general agreement that a lot of people regarded the blind as also defective in hearing and mind. There was the story of the man returning home, who said, "Yes, the V.A.D. found me a seat and went off. I said, 'Good morning', but all I got was bags of dead silence. I started to read my Braille book, and heard whispers—'see, he can read with his fingers', and there were other comments about the things I did. I decided to have my own bit of fun: carefully and unobtrusively I felt the time on my Braille watch in my pocket; then I drew it out with a flourish. I clicked open the metal cover and sniffed. Showing the watch to the person on my right, I announced for all and sundry, 'Twenty-two-minutes past two.' The gasps of incredulous astonishment made me feel the scales had been tilted in my favour."

Then there was the chap, travelling with his wife on a train, who went up the corridor to the toilet, but found it occupied. Rather than go back or explore further, he decided to wait, but the person occupying it was an inordinately long time. Thinking his wife would be wondering what was happening, he went back, and opened what he thought was the compartment where his wife was sitting just inside. He put his head round the door, and said quietly: "Somebody's died in the lavatory." The gasp of horror told him that he had mistaken the compartment, and that explanations were needed.

# CHAPTER 5

## THE LITTLE THINGS

During my first months in the R.A.F., when I was attending a disciplinary course as an N.C.O., the warrant officer in charge of the course had made a remark concerned with maintaining discipline which I still remember, finding it applicable in a much wider context: "It's the little things, Thornton, the little things!" In the early stages of learning to live with blindness, there were a whole host of little things which might produce acute frustration and "traumatic" experience.

Many blind people have found it such a problem to cope with food according to normal British conventions that they arrange for their food to be cut up, so that they can eat it using only a spoon and fork. This is probably safer on the whole than trying to develop a technique of using implements in the ordinary sighted manner. It is more likely to avoid embarrassing situations, and it means you have more freedom to concentrate on any conversation that's going. Then again, there are many people who very much like being helpful, and it gives them satisfaction—although I came to realise that sighted people don't always know what is likely to be troublesome and what is not: for instance, they expect a steak to be difficult, which it isn't if the knife is sharp, but don't grasp that lettuce can be most unmanageable.

In any case, having your food cut up causes a sense of restriction and restraint. It means you need special attention; somebody else's food may get cold while he deals with yours; and on other occasions it can cause delays which are themselves a source of embarrassment. So on balance I decided I would try to evolve a technique of coping with the food myself. One useful thing about this exercise was that I developed the tactile sense for using instruments, which I am sure has proved a valuable faculty generally.

At first I would ask someone to say roughly where the various foods on my plate were, using the clock system for target indication, for example: "Meat at twelve o'clock, potatoes at six, peas at three, celery at nine." But this didn't take me very far, because the different items soon got mixed up. I also found I had to be constantly on my guard against a tendency to pull the food towards the near edge of the plate—peas have always remained a particular menace in this respect. With my intimates I developed an early-warning system, by which they would say "five o'clock" or "six o'clock" to give the area of the plate where there was a danger of something coming over the edge—so that I could push it back towards the middle.

I learned, too, to beware of specially difficult foods, like lettuce— already mentioned—which I usually avoid altogether or try to cut into small pieces before starting to eat. Clear soup also needs special concentration, so I always opt for a thick soup when there is a choice. If I am to avoid difficulties, I still have to give some attention to the mechanics of controlling my knife and fork, and to checking that the food is not approaching the edge of my plate.

When you are picking up a glass or some other vessel containing liquid, some people advocate slowly sliding your hand from the edge of the table towards the target. This, even in my early days, seemed to me a movement fraught with hazards. It was surely safer to raise your hand in a natural manner, extending the fingers as you did so in a movement towards where you expected the cup or glass to be, and to approach it from above. I got on very well with this method, although I learnt later on that tall lager glasses, or other special glasses, could be troublesome because they were taller than the usual height of approach by the hand. However, you could usually expect some warning of this difficulty beforehand.

The period between being allowed up at Stoke Mandeville and returning to Church Stretton at the beginning of January 1946 was probably the most intensive in my search for answers to the little problems of everyday life created by my blindness. As I have said, I found many useful hints in Sir Ian Fraser's book *Whereas I was Blind*, some of which were common sense once you knew them, but mightn't occur at once to the newly blinded person.

For instance, it was clearly easier to get about with an escort if you took her arm (rather than the other way round) and walked slightly behind. The value of having your hand placed on the back of a chair was immediately obvious: it simplified the process of making sure you sat down without awkwardness or incident. So far as I remember, however, Sir Ian did not mention first making sure the chair *has* a back if the person you are with does not indicate it. I learnt this lesson when I tried to lean back on a park bench which ought to have had a back but didn't.

In dealing with money, I found coins easy enough; our British coinage might have been designed so that you could distinguish it by touch as well as sight, the milled edge showing silver coins of higher denomination. Notes were more difficult, until I realised you could carry out a quick unobtrusive check by passing the note through the first and second fingers, measuring it against the index finger while doing so. To make assurance doubly sure, I followed a careful practice of always keeping notes of different values in opposite sides of my wallet; a piece of stiff card in the pound-note side helped to avoid any risk of confusion.

A template, cut to fit my cheque book, enabled me to write out my own cheques if I wished. This was the driving force at the time: to satisfy myself that I could, if necessary, do unaided whatever had to be done. The books of stamps then on sale contained stamps of different denominations. I learned the sequence and number of pages for the different values of stamps, and tore off the top right-hand corner of the front of the book to make the process of recognition easier. When I wished to send postcards, I arranged for the stamps to be put on when I bought the cards. I covered the message part of the card while writing the address, and similarly covered the address part while writing the message. I was so determined not to lose the ability to write in long-hand that I made myself do a daily period of writing, although I did not show it to anybody.

Dialling numbers on the telephone was a laborious matter if you used only the index finger and counted each number round the dial. The use of all four fingers made things a good deal easier. With the little finger in the space for number 1 you only had to move the index finger forward one space to cover the first five digits. The other five could be covered in the same way by placing the little finger in the zero space, and moving the index finger one space forward to reach the six. Dialling exchanges with letters was more of a business. You had to remember that the letters started in the number 2 space, and to memorise the arrangement of the letters in consecutive groups of three, apart from two, M and N, which occurred in the number 6 space. To convert a letter exchange into the numbers I wished to dial, I counted on my fingers, keeping down the fingers which represented the number of the exchange. This needed a good deal of effort, particularly in memorising an unfamiliar number, but came more easily with practice. Much later on, I learned to dial with the left hand whilst reading Braille numbers with the right; I held the receiver against my ear by wedging it under the lapel of my jacket.

I realised the need to lighten the load for everyday living by reducing wherever possible the demands on memory or concentration. If I kept to my own tooth-paste, I could gauge the quantity to be used much more easily by putting the end of the tube in my mouth and squeezing a little out instead of trying to measure it along the toothbrush. I could avoid the risk of confusing brushless shaving cream with tooth-paste by always buying them in different sizes. The same applied to hair cream bought in the tube.

I avoided the possibility of using black shoe polish on brown shoes by keeping the equipment in different places. I at first avoided the danger of mixing up shoes—wearing one black and one brown— by buying shoes of different styles. To match ties and socks to suits, I had an arrangement in my wardrobe for separating sports suits and accessories from more formal clothes.

It was a satisfaction to know that there were games such as cards, chess and dominoes, which you could play with pieces distinguishable by touch. In the case of cards, Braille symbols were embossed for identification. The white pieces in chess had points, the black being smooth; the black squares of the chess-board were raised. Dominoes simply had raised dots instead of spots which could not be felt. I had always enjoyed a game of snooker, and tried it again, but reluctantly decided it couldn't be done without putting far too big a burden on my partner.

There were little jobs I could help with in the house, like washing up or making the morning tea. Approaching with the hand from above proved as effective a safety measure in washing up when you wished to locate the article of crockery to be picked up, as at the table when locating your glass. If there was no undue noise around, you could tell by sound whether or not the kettle was boiling; but in any case there was no risk attached to passing the hand quickly across the line of the spout to see whether steam was issuing, so long as you felt the handle with your other hand in order to know, by gauging the distance, where the spout was. It has proved a useful habit always to point a kettle in the same direction when putting it on to boil.

In pouring the water into the teapot, or the tea into the teacups, you could tell by sound if you had poured in enough; though again you could make mistakes because of ambient noise or through lack of concentration. When pouring milk out of the bottle, you could tell how full it was by feeling the weight, and this would be a guide on how far to tilt the bottle when pouring the milk into a jug or cup. When walking through a doorway carrying a tray with cups, or carrying my baby daughter, I adopted the technique of backing through so that there could be no chance of dangerous collision.

Perhaps one of the biggest gains of this period was the way I learned to rely on my remaining senses to give me accurate and reliable information, even sometimes when my sighted friends made statements apparently at variance with my own observations. Hard practice was sharpening my hearing, obviously the sense I now had to rely on most; and I found I was noticing sounds which went unnoticed by those who relied largely on sight to tell them about their environment.

Once, for instance, following a friend up a linoleum-covered staircase, I heard a tinkle as a coin dropped to the floor. I said to him: "I think you've dropped a sixpence." "Really?" he said, "I don't think I have." I suggested he should look on the staircase, and there it was. He then examined his trouser pocket, and found a small hole the coin had dropped through.

On another occasion, when a friend called at home to see us, I thought I had caught the end of my cigarette as I went through the lounge from the hall where some coats were hanging. I was afraid the cigarette end might be smouldering, but the family had a look and decided I must be mistaken; they pointed out that my cigarette was still alight. I sat there for a minute or two, feeling more and more uncomfortable, and convinced that I had not been mistaken. I suggested they should have another look, and this time they saw smoke rising from inside an overcoat pocket, into which the bit of burning end had dropped; luckily, not too much damage had been done. I told myself I must make it second nature to keep my senses active at all times, and try to get the maximum information from them.

Towneley Hall, an Elizabethan country house, was a few minutes' walk from our house in Burnley. For many years it has been the town museum and its grounds a public park. It had always been a favourite spot of ours, and during the Christmas break Margaret and I often walked there. It was all so familiar that I did not feel the loss of sight: the curve or slope of the paths told me exactly where we were, so that I knew the immediate landscape or distant view; the remoter parts of the park had the same soothing stillness and serenity, and the crunch of the leaves underfoot was the same memory-filled sound that it had always been.

I was very much aware of the difficulties Margaret was facing. My life was filled with a succession of problems to solve, but I was spared the sight of what I looked like with my scars, closed left eye, and right eye removed—although I was often greatly embarrassed to overhear noises and remarks made by tactless if kind-hearted people as I walked by. Margaret had to watch my struggles, suffer the livelier embarrassment of my mistakes, the gaffes I committed, the awkward moments I inevitably produced. She also had to restrain her instinct to help when I was trying to recover some sort of practical ability, and had to sit at home waiting for me to return when I went out walking on my own.

I said I expected she would find it embarrassing on occasions when I wanted to examine objects with my hands, perhaps in a shop, a friend's house, or some place of interest we might be visiting. This was one of the ways in which I could once again get a real and accurate impression of my environment, a need I felt acutely. Verbal descriptions would undoubtedly help, and would often have to do, but could not really give that vividness of impression which comes through the senses. It was a great support to me that Margaret accepted this without question, and that, though she often felt torn by the claims of our baby daughter and my needs, she contrived to remain cheerful, practical and uncomplaining. As the time drew near for me to return to Church Stretton, I felt we had made a good deal of genuine progress.

# CHAPTER 6

## LAST MONTHS AT CHURCH STRETTON

The remaining six months which I spent at Church Stretton developed, with variations, the theme of the first three. The programme of training remained much the same, but the use of the Braille writing frame, shorthand, and Braille music, were added to my syllabus. Up to now, I had used only the Stainsby Wayne Braille writing machine. This consists of three parts: a device to hold in position the large sheets of paper, twelve inches by sixteen; a frame the paper is threaded through, which holds the moving carriage containing the embossing unit; and the plate this frame rests on. There are holes down each side of the plate with pegs fitting into them on the underside of the frame, thus keeping it in position during the writing process.

You write by pressing on one or more of six keys arranged in two vertical rows of three, corresponding to the arrangement of the dots in a single Braille cell. The embossing unit moves along as the keys are pressed, and springs raise the keys for the next pressure. The action of the embossing unit is downwards, which has certain disadvantages. The writer cannot examine what he has written without taking the paper out of the frame and turning it over. Because the paper has to be turned over in order to be read, writing is done from right to left. The letter "a" is written by depressing the top left-hand key. The design of the machine has not been very much altered since it was first introduced in 1900, and it is still preferred by many who have adapted themselves to its limitations and got used to its noisiness.

Some confusion was produced by the introduction of the hand-frame Braille writer. There are several types of these, but the essential difference from the machines is that you produce the Braille characters by pushing a stylus through the paper from above, using a metal guide to locate the position of the dots. A cut-out rectangle in the frame indicates one cell, and depressions in the base plate give the precise position of the dots and act as a female die against the tip of the stylus.

The difficulty and source of confusion for somebody like myself, a comparative new-comer to Braille, was that the single dot representing the letter "a" now had to be written at the top of the right-hand column instead of at the top of the left. The embossing unit of the Stainsby Wayne machine is so arranged that the position of the keys which you depressed conformed to the arrangement of a Braille cell as you read it. With the hand-frame, this was not possible. You had to substitute right for left while making the writing depressions, which meant you had to turn certain letters round and shift the position of others from the left side to the right.

You wrote the letter "I", for instance, so that when the paper was turned over, it could be read as the letter "E", the letter "H" became a "J", and so on. To read the word "of" you had to write "with", and vice versa. To read the word "the" you had to write the letter "Z", while "Y" became "and". Again, the first ten letters of the Braille alphabet are used to indicate the numbers one to zero, and they have a numeral sign before them to show they are to be read as numbers. When you used the hand-frame, this meant that what was written as five was read as nine, nine became five, six became four, and so on.

Even now, twenty years later, I still find I have sometimes to make a conscious effort to remember which way round to write when using my pocket hand-frame; and research might usefully be carried out to discover how long should be allowed to a person learning Braille before the complication of using the hand-frame is introduced. The pocket hand-frame is a tremendously valuable aid. The one I still use was given to me by one of the Canadian V.A.D.s, Morna Barclay. Made of an aluminium alloy, it is about six and a half inches long, and three inches wide, and has six rows of eighteen cells each. It acts as a notebook.

The machine on which I learned to write Braille shorthand, produced by the Royal National Institute for the Blind, is still, so far as I know, the best of its kind in the world. A reel of paper an inch wide is fed through a guide containing the embossing unit, which is operated by six keys placed in line abreast, with a spacing between the left and right-hand sets of three. The same fingers are used as with the Stainsby Wayne, so that there is no danger of getting mixed up between them. A weight screws into the bar connecting the keys, spacer, and embossing unit. This provides the force which returns the keys to position and also moves the paper along, retaining rollers at each end of the paper guide assisting this process. Although other Braille shorthand writers might have difficulty in reading the system which I evolved, this training and machine have been of great benefit to me.

At this time I was trying to improve my reading and writing speeds, and also my accuracy and speed in typing. In peacetime my instructor, Tommy Milligan, an ex-Guardsman, had a job in the City as a shorthand typist, but I did not need his comments to make me put away any idea of looking for a similar job; although I realised that I would probably have to be prepared to accept almost anything as a start. Some of the officers had been moved to another house, Southview, higher up Sandford Avenue, and I now had a room to myself; so I was not likely to disturb anyone if I filled some of the night hours when I couldn't sleep reading Braille. It seemed also to act as a mental tranquiliser, perhaps because it was tiring; so that it often served as a means of getting me off to sleep again.

Progress with learning Braille music was very limited, and none of Claude Bampton's three pupils kept it up. All that remains from that particular attempt is that "MUVX", symbol for a long rest in music, was used for a time as a variant for less polite expressions like "wrap up" or "belt up".

People still had their misadventures with the typewriter, not always caused by the vagaries of a communal machine. One of the newer admissions, Peter Matthews, told us one day that he had just written a letter to his wife, but had forgotten to put in the paper, and so had typed his letter on the roller. We suggested he should post the roller, and get his wife to rotate it in front of a mirror.

It was also Peter who made another amusing typing slip. Padre

Nugee had had the good idea that it would be helpful for some of us to get practice in listening to a reader, with checks on what we had absorbed in the way of factual information. We were to listen to readings at speed, and then type out a summary of the essential matter. Peter had written, "In her essay on Liberalism, Dame Megan Lloyd George says"; and having put the shift-key down to write the quotation marks, had resumed on the wrong bank of the typewriter. The result was an unintelligible jumble, which the person checking Peter's summary mistook for Welsh, as Peter had got back on to the right bank of the typewriter after using the shift key once again for the closing quotation marks!

When not receiving instruction I spent a good deal of time with Margaret and Catherine at the lodgings in Watling Street where they were still staying. The arrangement was not very satisfactory, because the accommodation consisted of only a bedroom, which was fiercely cold when the snow came, and it was also evident that the lady of the house expected the baby never to cry. The Nugees, with whom we had become friendly, offered to have Margaret and the baby, and I shall always remember our arrival. Mrs. Nugee was leading the way up the rather long flight of stairs which led straight up from the entrance hall. Margaret was carrying Catherine, who was holding her feeding bottle. Suddenly Catherine decided that she had held the bottle long enough, and threw it. It hit the tiled floor of the passage below, flew through the open door of the study, and hit the opposite wall—luckily it did not break.

This period at "Langdale" was a happy one. The Nugees loved children, and Catherine was even accepted by their dog, Sammy, who normally resented any interference with his way of life, particularly if it involved his special seat, a nicety which Catherine was much too young to recognise.

Romance was quite common in those days, and as it happened to be very wet just then, some wit converted the address "Church Stretton, near Much Wenlock, Salop" into "Church Wetton, by Much Wedlock, Slop". I had had my suspicions during one of our visits to Chelmick with its non-austerity fare, when Marjorie Pitt-Watson's attention seemed to be devoted almost exclusively to

keeping Ted Barton's plate filled. The suspicions were stimulated a
little more when Marjorie came up the stairs at Southview singing,
"Oh, don't deceive me, Oh, never leave me", etc. The engagement was
announced a day or two later. On the day after the announcement
we were walking down Sandford Avenue together to the Training
Centre. Somehow a race developed between Ted and me. Our walking
pace quickened, and we broke into a run, discretion almost thrown
to the winds. Marjorie ran behind us, shouting "Stop, stop", as we
headed towards the by-pass with its military traffic. We did stop in
time, both feeling exhilarated by the sudden feeling of freedom
from restraint. This was something Ted and I had discussed once or
twice.

"You know, Wally," he said, "there are times when I forget I'm
blind. Then I do something stupid and the truth really comes home."

We agreed we just couldn't go around all the time reminding ourselves that we couldn't see. We agreed, too, that the answer was to
develop habits which would make self-protection an automatic
process. If we moved about quickly and carelessly, even indoors
in familiar surroundings, we were bound to crack our shins against
a low piece of furniture, or our heads against a half-open door. I
thought of a picture from my childhood of a blind man with his
arms stretched out in front of him. That surely wasn't necessary. You
could look a good deal more natural than that and still be protected,
if you held your arm across the body, the hand resting about
trouser-top level. Outside, we still collected the occasional bump,
but there didn't seem any way of avoiding this.

Another remark of Ted's which stuck was when, strumming his
guitar one day, he suddenly said: "Blind people give me the willies."
He seemed to be looking at me as he made this pronouncement, and
I thought for a moment he was being personal. We had talked before
about jobs that might be done by blind people, about sheltered
occupations and community workshops. I gathered that this cryptic
remark was meant to indicate that what he wanted was to lead a
normal life in a normal community, and that he regarded the sort of
life we were leading as necessary for a time but one to be ended as
soon as possible.

"Yes," I said. "Same here. I suppose it's a matter of temperament. Perhaps we're not gregarious enough or maybe we just want to be more independent. I haven't a clue what I'm going to do when I leave here, but whatever it is, I want it to be something I can do as well as the next bloke, sighted or not."

Ted changed the subject by singing to his guitar a somewhat derogatory song of his own composition about one of the lady helpers whose attentions he found too gushing.

Jobs one might do was an infrequent but absorbing topic of conversation. I had discussed it with Geoff Preston, an Army officer, who had been blown up, and who, besides being totally blinded, had lost a right hand. Shrapnel lodged in his brain more or less paralysed his left side, so that he had a perfectly good left hand which he could not use. By the time I shared a room with him during my first three months at Church Stretton, Geoff had passed through the Slough of Despond and the Valley of Despair, and was a splendid example of the real spirit of St. Dunstan's, not yet triumphant, but unconquerable.

He had confided to me something of what he had been through on his way back to this country, but it was others who told me of the determination he had shown in making the most of what he had, in struggling for months to learn to open a door for himself, in learning to type, and in walking about unaided. I was fascinated by the sound of his typing; it was a series of clickety clicks, interspersed by plonks, with the less frequent variant of the sound of the paper being turned up. His typewriter keyboard was fitted with a metal cover, and there were holes immediately above the keys. In a leather strap round his right wrist he had fixed an L-shaped piece of metal. The "clickety clicks" were produced by this being run across the line of the keys, and the "plonks" as he came to the right key and pressed.

At one point Geoff thought he might become a bookmaker. He had a good knowledge of the Turf, and mathematical ability. He didn't pursue this idea, because he found he could sell the crossword puzzles which he was already devising. His system was to memorise the pattern of the puzzle, think up his clues and answers, and type them out. To date, he has produced over five thousand of these.

At Battlefield our beds were in opposite corners of the same room, and we would play chess: I had the board and pieces, and moved the pieces as indicated. I always lost!

When I told Geoff I had wondered about going back to teaching, he commented: "You can't do that. It wouldn't be fair to the little devils. They would be on their honour all the time."

I was inclined to agree with him, but for other reasons. I knew there had been many successful blind teachers, but I had forgotten a good deal of what I had learned, and had declined Sir Ian Fraser's suggestion that I might take another degree, as I felt I wanted to support my family and should not be tied to a three-year course of study. Before the war I had hoped to move from teaching into educational administration, and had started to work for an external degree in Law towards that end; I wondered whether this might still be possible. A good friend of St. Dunstan's put into Braille for me the 1944 Education Act, which I still retain as a treasured possession; but reading it helped to convince me that I would be wise to abandon any ideas of educational administration. For the time being I decided to adopt the philosophy of Mr. Micawber: something would turn up.

I was still trying to improve my technique in getting around. Although I didn't get very much information through the medium of my feet, I had observed that the camber of the road varied considerably in different parts of the village. I mentioned this at the luncheon table, and somebody suggested that I carried in my pocket a piece of adjustable camber to put against the road's surface which would tell me where I was. There had been some talk of an aid to mobility in the shape of an obstacle detector, a device produced by Professor R. L. Beurle of Nottingham University. Ted Barton and I were asked to try it out and report on our findings.

It was impressed on us that we had to take extreme care of the apparatus, and at all costs must not go crashing into anything with it. It was a large box which you strapped to the chest. Batteries were carried in the pocket, and an audible signal was heard through an earpiece. A beam of light went out from the middle of the box. The idea was that this would be reflected back from objects in one's path, and a photo-electric cell device would activate the audible signal. We decided we would take it in turns to carry the apparatus, the other man going ahead to discover obstacles, so that the carrier could "find" them without danger of bumping the apparatus. Approaching the Training Centre along Sandford Avenue, Ted suddenly stopped.

"There's something here, Wally," he announced.

There was. It was Tony, one of our readers, who was watching our antics in some amazement.

I heard Ted's stick swish.

"Ow," exclaimed Tony.

We laughed our apologies, explained that we were trying out a gadget, and went on our way.

We had to report that, while we welcomed attention to the production of such devices, we did not think it compared in efficiency and effectiveness with the walking-stick. One of the chief snags was that its operation was adversely affected by sunlight. However, it seemed to point the way towards future development which might be really helpful.

An amusing outcome of this trial was that Squadron Leader Simpson, author of One of our Pilots is Safe and The Way of Recovery, who was doing some journalistic work, came to talk to us about our experience with the device. We adjourned to The Plough, and ordered our beers. Although Simpson had lost some of his fingers, and found it difficult to drink from an ordinary glass, it was necessary to point this out to mine host, who had provided glass mugs with handles for "the boys", but the ordinary type for our sighted friend. This kind of special treatment was sometimes embarrassing. It shows the ready sympathy which blindness evokes in all classes and ages and, so far as my experience goes, in all races. The reverse seems to be the case with deafness, which appears to provoke irritation rather than sympathy. We used to talk about this, and felt that the loss of human contact must be a sore trial for the deaf.

Simpson had some amusing stories about his experiences. One concerned his travelling on a London bus after he had had his sequence of plastic surgery operations. The conductor was obviously sympathetic and studiously ignored the proffered fare. As Simpson was getting off the bus he said to him, "Been in the wars, Guv?" "That's right." "Tell you what, Guv," said the conductor, looking at Simpson's scarred face, "You ought to see one of them plastic surgeons, they work miracles!"

Although I felt I was making progress towards rehabilitation, there were days when things got on top of me—and it was the same with most of the others. This may have made us irritable at times with people who tried in well-meaning but misguided ways to help. It was humiliating when someone convinced he knew how to deal with the blind seized you by the shoulders from behind and propelled you forward, or tried to lift you into a chair. It was also somewhat galling to meet people who did not address you directly, but addressed your escort as if you were not there, or if acknowledged to be there, regarded as a sort of mental defective. "Does he take sugar?" epitomises this kind of reaction to blindness.

The lesson which came through, perhaps more slowly than it should, is that the onus of responsibility in receiving help lies with the blind person, to see that he gets the help in the way most suitable. He has far more experience of dealing with sighted people than they have of dealing with the blind. Gradual education of the general public is the only hope of converting to a more sensible view the people who think that because someone is blind he must be half-witted and deaf as well. Tommy Milligan, balanced and tolerant, had a helpful comment, as usual: "You'll find sometimes that when people offer to help you in the street, they are looking for a chance to have a chat with you."

This led Tommy to reminisce about some of the things which had happened to him when going about alone.

"The funniest, I think, was in the old Regent's Park days of St. Dunstan's. I was ambling slowly across the front of the building, not taking much notice, and rather lost in my thoughts. Suddenly something whipped up from between my legs, and threw me on my back. There was a funny champing sound ahead of me. For a moment I was baffled, and then I realised what had happened. I had walked astride a horse with its head down in its nosebag. It had lifted its head to get rid of the encumbrance, and had then got on with its dinner. I was glad it hadn't got scared or it might have run over me."

The summer term came, and we were blessed with warm fine days which reflected the bright news of the war's progress. It was clear that the war in Europe was drawing to a close, and that the problems of the peace would soon be upon us. We had discussed these matters with visiting panels doing a sort of "Any Questions" act. We had even formed our own panel, which had made similar appearances at A.T.S. units in the area, and we were amused to receive certificates declaring that we had assisted with educational work in the Western Command area. From the world outside we heard that Bill Robinson was doing a personnel job with I.C.I. in Northwich, and that Ted Barton was in Huddersfield applying his talents to the problems of chemical engineering.

With an increase in our numbers we had been moved once again, this time to a former preparatory school, Brockhurst, a mile or so outside the village. It was beyond the gasworks, the point at which the men going to their billet in Longmynd Hotel said, "You sniffs and you turns right." Brockhurst had a drive about a hundred yards long, and its situation meant that those who wanted to make their own way to the Training Centre would, willy nilly, be given more practice in getting about. It also meant that the less mobile, like Geoff Preston, were rather out of things. There was only the one celebrated occasion when we decided to take Geoff out for a drink at The Plough. We must have looked rather funny as we progressed along the road, clustered round him like destroyers round a battle-ship. We made the return journey in safety, although we only knew one side of the road; but we had to come back on the opposite side, because Geoff only had one good side we could steer him by.

In our new quarters I shared a room with Tommy Claxton and Peter Matthews. Tommy was still officially in the Navy, and seemed likely to continue so for an indefinite period. Peter was planning to return to his old job of estate management, and I felt he was lucky to have got his line worked out. He was reading the Uthwatt report as part of his vocational preparation, and I was amused one day to overhear an atrocious pun of his when his reader asked what they should do that afternoon: "Uthwatt you like, Cecil."

Peter and I made various expeditions together. There was a place of refreshment we had been to in Ash's Valley, which lay across the fields. We obtained information about the route, and decided we would try to get there one evening. There should be no difficulty about crossing the fields since there were two of us, and one could stay put while the other found the exit at the other side of the field. It all went without incident. We crossed the bridge to the catering establishment, entered, climbed the stairs, and gave our order as though this type of evening outing were a common occurrence.

In Church Stretton's peaceful streets the hazards were few; you could normally rely on detecting by echo the occasional parked vehicle, although once I memorably failed to do so. Peter and I were walking back to Brockhurst after the morning's instructional session. We had discovered a route through the fields which avoided a good deal of Sandford Avenue and the High Street. It brought us out near the King's Arms towards the end of the village. We had turned into the High Street, and there seemed to be nothing about. "I think we can step out now, Peter," I said, and did so, stopping with a loud thump as I walked into the back of a small van; the timing couldn't have been improved on by the most expert film director. Peter thought it killing, perhaps because for once he wasn't the victim; and after a moment or two, somewhat ruefully, I joined in his laughter.

On another occasion we went to visit my former Braille teacher, Miss Dewing, who was ill. It was an entirely new route, but we made our enquiries, and decided we could find the place. We did, and marched up the drive silently congratulating ourselves. Casting around to find the entrance to the house, I caught my head very forcibly against a protruding beam, and once again had to remind myself that the final stages in any enterprise, great or small, are just as vital as any of the other stages, and that a blind person can never afford to relax the vigilance, alertness and concentration which are his safeguard if he chooses to walk alone. When we left Miss Dewing, we found we had been a good deal longer than we had thought.

If we walked back to Brockhurst, we should miss tea, and that was unthinkable. There was only one hope, that a car would come along and we could hitch a lift. We managed to do so, and felt we had added another to the list of little things we could do if we wanted.

Another new arrival at Church Stretton was Squadron Leader Norton Christal, blinded on bomb-disposal work with the R.A.F. Before the war he had been a master at King William's College, in the Isle of Man, and he was planning to return there. As I had passed the various Braille tests and was now trying to improve my speed, it was proposed that I might help a little with one or two whose Braille was at a more elementary stage. At the time Norton was living with his wife, Betty, and young son at the home of the Bursar, Squadron Leader Bartlett, who had a spaniel dog which had attached itself to Norton. We met as usual at the Centre one morning, and went to the little room backstage in the large hut used for entertainments and dances. As we sat down and turned to our Braille books, I thought I heard a slight noise in the corner of the room. I reminded myself that I had to be prepared to trust the evidence of my senses. Somebody had made that noise.

"Hullo," I said. "Who's there?"

There was no reply.

"Funny do this, Norton," I said. "I'll swear I heard somebody just then."

"Somebody's playing the fool," we decided. Norton said he would stand by the door while I explored the room. I moved round systematically covering the sides of the room, and swishing my stick as I went. Suddenly there was a yelp as my stick caught the backside of the Bursar's dog, which, unknown to Norton, had followed him from the house.

My principal recreations during these last months at Church Stretton were riding, walking, playing the piano, dancing—and conversation. Riding around the region was almost as good as walking for getting the feel of its hills and valleys, and it was a joy to experience the windswept freshness of the summit of Caradoc, or gallop across the springy turf of Ash's Valley. Although my piano playing was for personal enjoyment only, I gained satisfaction from the simple tunes which were my sum of performance, and on occasions when frustration and despondency seemed to bite into the soul, I got a kind of catharsis from playing it, however unskilfully. Fortunately for the peace of others, the pianos at Brockhurst and the Training Centre were away from the centre of things. There did not seem to be much time to listen to the wireless, but it was obviously the blind man's friend, and potentially a fruitful source of information and enjoyment.

Braille-reading still remained something of a chore, although I managed to enjoy the two detective stories I read.

Most of us took part in the athletic sports which were held on the Brockhurst playing field. I took part in the standing long jump and the timed sprint towards a sound guide. It was the first, and almost the last time that I ran full speed for any distance as a blind person. It was an interesting experience, but not one I was particularly anxious to repeat. It seemed to me that the concentration of keeping in line with the sound guide reduced the pleasure one might have expected to feel from running freely and without restraint. Although I had no interest or ability in "walking racing", I thought that this, with an escort, would be a much more satisfying branch of athletic activity for the blind. Rowing, which we did not do at Church Stretton because of transport difficulties, seemed also an activity which a blind person with a cox would be able to perform as adequately as his sighted competitor.

On a few occasions some of the chaps from Brockhurst went playing golf. As I had played only a few games of golf in my life, I was not tempted to join them, particularly as it seemed to me that the totally blind player would need an inordinate amount of assistance when playing. It is a different proposition, I think, for anyone who can see enough to discern the ball without having to touch it to know where it is. Games like croquet and bowls seem much more possible, and I wonder if sets of balls might not be produced for these games with built-in sound transmitters. I tried my hand at table tennis, but found that although serving was easy enough I could rarely hit my opponent's return.

On the whole I felt that ball games were "out", and that there were far less frustrating fields of activity such as swimming, diving, gymnastics, wrestling and judo—where contact with your environment was an essential part of the activity. Skating seemed just as possible as ballroom dancing. Some blind people ski very well, I was told, and I am a bit sorry that I have never tried it; although I should imagine the type of skiing they do must be restricted by "navigation problems".

# CHAPTER 7

SEEKING EMPLOYMENT

About the time of the Sports, dissatisfaction with myself for not being able to decide the line I wanted to follow seemed to boil up. I had wondered about physiotherapy, a profession in which the blinded of the First World War had done so well, but somehow didn't think it was for me. I had toyed with the idea of becoming a shopkeeper, and reckoned it would not be beyond me, although I had no experience of trade. I felt, however, that this would involve the family, and considered it was up to me to find something I could do on my own. Since I did not want to spend a long time undergoing training, and since I possessed neither special skills nor knowledge, apart from the teaching which I did not wish to do, one of the few things left seemed to be some form of social work.

I don't think there was anything wrong with me physically, but I got myself into such a state that I developed a kind of fever and was actually ordered to bed for a day or two. I spent part of the time applying for a post as a community centre organiser in Nottingham, but did not even get an acknowledgement of my application. At one point I seemed to have the chance of working for St. Dunstan's but then the prospective offer was withdrawn, and this did not help. I stopped going to The Plough with my fellows, because my stomach nerves seemed all churned up and the thought of beer was anathema.

Mr. Small, the Placements Officer, came on one of his regular visits. There was the possibility of a job with the Ministry of Pensions, which would involve being centred on Stoke Mandeville Hospital. The Civil Service was something I had not thought of, and I wondered what the chances of promotion might be. Somehow I didn't really fancy the limitations of being a civil servant, but a job was a job, and a friend whose advice I valued recommended applying. Paul Baker, who had been in Stoke Mandeville at the same time as me, also decided to apply, and we travelled with Mr. Small to Blackpool for the interview. In my brief-case I carried a Braille book, a sample of my typing and handwriting, the template for my cheque book, and my Braille pocket frame.

We arrived at the County Hotel in time for lunch, and learnt that we were not to be interviewed by Captain X as expected, but by Mr. Y deputising for him. I had left my brief-case in the cloak-room, and wondered whether to get out the Braille frame and cheque template, but for some reason decided not to bother.

When we were introduced to Mr. Y, he told us almost at once that he had started as a temporary civil servant and was now a four-figure man. I took an instant dislike to him, which increased when he spotted a prominent politician who happened to be in the room and made a great parade of introducing us. It was clear from his attitude that the Ministry was handing out charity: something had to be done for these blind chaps, even though they would be a permanent liability. The interview was short and hostile; I have often wondered if things might have gone differently with Captain X.

I thought Mr. Y was a small-minded jack-in-office, and was damned if I would adopt the subservient manner he clearly expected of me. He said that of course I would need to be led round, and obviously disbelieved me when I told him I had got round Stoke Mandeville Hospital on my own almost as soon as I was allowed to get up. When I asked about the prospects of promotion, he was equally sceptical about a blind man producing the memoranda required of a civil servant in the administrative grade.

"Squire" Goodwin, an excise officer blinded while serving in the Dover area, offered friendly words of sympathy on my return to Brockhurst: no doubt something better would turn up; maybe things had gone the way they had because I knew underneath that I didn't really want the job. Paul took the position, however, and although he didn't stay in it very long—he changed over to physio-therapy—I didn't know that at the time, and reproached myself for being stupid and hyper-sensitive.

Bill Robinson had gone into personnel work in industry, which I thought sounded challenging, though I hadn't much idea what the work really amounted to. Elizabeth Nugee, who was helping as a reader, read me one or two pamphlets produced by one of the industrial societies; and also G. S. Walpole's *Management and Men*, a recent book on joint consultation. I felt this was both a fascinating field and something I could hope to tackle.

Despite my interest I fell asleep one hot afternoon when Elizabeth was reading to me, as we sat in deck-chairs on the lawn at the back of the house. When I woke up, I was alone: she had decided she might as well go in and get on with some household chores. I suppose I was both tired and short of sleep at the time, and she showed her usual good temper, although it must have seemed distinctly rude; but I still remember my acute embarrassment when I woke and realised what had happened: I have never known a place feel so empty.

I was less bothered by a similar experience about the same time—with my old C.O. at Regent's Park, Group Captain Locke, who had been made C.O. of R.A.F. Bridgnorth. He came to see me, and invited me to go over and have lunch with him. I was delighted, and a few days later a car collected me and took me to Bridgnorth. It was a pleasant lunch, we sat out on the lawn afterwards in the sun, chatting with some of the other members of the Mess; and again I fell asleep. I received much chaff when they woke me, but didn't mind this time. Evidently the Group Captain didn't either, because he drove me back himself to Brockhurst.

Fairly soon I got on to Mr. Small again. I was feeling pretty fed up and charged him with not doing as much for me as he might have done. "Look, what about this personnel line?" I said. "Why not try one of those firms like Cadbury's, who I hear do a lot of this sort of thing?"

I don't know if this stirred him to action, or if he had already been making enquiries; but quite soon afterwards he and I were making another railway journey together, this time to Birmingham.

As we came out of Snow Hill Station, I could smell the dirt in the atmosphere. This was very different from the pure air of Shropshire, which seemed to make walking up the hills light work, even for the oldest inhabitants. Ah well, I thought, where there's muck, there's money, and I want to earn my living.

Our appointment was for two-thirty, so after having some lunch we clattered out on a tram along the Bristol and Pershore Roads to The British Oak, where we had been told to get out. As we walked along Bournville Lane, I said: "Surely this part can't be Bourneville—this is no model village, is it?"

Mr. Small agreed, and supplemented the impression I had gained of my surroundings. We went under a railway bridge, walking one behind the other on the narrow footpath. As we came though, he said: "There we are. That looks better." Ahead of us on the right were the factory buildings, and there was a small stone building skirting the footpath. "I reckon this must be number one Lodge."

The lodge-keeper was cheery and polite. He told us where we should find the Men's Employment Office, and we passed through the lodge, down a few steps, and across a yard.

"Nice little garden here," said Mr. Small; and I thought: this is more like what I expected. We went down a steep flight of stone steps, and found ourselves in the office. From behind a counter someone asked what he could do for us. "You have an appointment to see Mr. Watts? He's busy at a meeting. Will you sit down and wait?"

We sat on a bench against the wall, the counter a yard or so away. The people behind the counter got on with their work, and the feeling I had of being someone without identity heightened. It was a feeling effectively suggested by the clerk who had asked our business: here were just a couple more drops in the stream that went through the place. We had arrived punctually. A quarter of an hour passed and nobody came near us. "Do you think they've forgotten we're here?" I asked Mr. Small. "Oh no," he said. "The meeting's still going on. Anyhow it's not a bad thing to be kept waiting when you're asking for something. It tends to put the other chap on the wrong foot, because he has something to apologise for."

The idea seemed sound, but I still felt as insignificant and anonymous as ever.

Just then a person who was evidently fairly senior in the office came up to the counter. "Hullo," he said. "My name's Jack White. I'm Mr. Watts's assistant. Have you just come up from Church Stretton this morning?" His voice was friendly, and had a quality of understanding about it which I recognised immediately. Obviously people matter to him, I thought. We chatted easily for a few minutes. "This meeting will soon be over," he said. "I'm sorry you're having to wait so long, but one can't always tell what's going to happen. I expect Mr. Watts will be taking you to meet Mr. Gillett. He's one of the directors."

This was better. Maybe I wasn't after all going to be treated like something the wind had blown in. "Ah," said Mr. White, "it looks as though the meeting is breaking up. I hope things go well for you." We shook hands and he returned to his desk.

A moment or two later Mr. Watts came out of his office, and walked over to the counter. He was pleasant but non-committal, and his voice had an edge of authority to it. "I'll see if Mr. Gillett can see you now," he said, and after a brief telephone call, got somebody to show us back across the yard into another building and to a small office.

"Ah, it's Mr. Small and Mr. Thornton," said the occupant before we had a chance to say anything. "Mr. Gillett is expecting you, and won't keep you a minute. Will you sit down?" She sounded genuinely friendly, and I thought: "Things get better; hope it continues this way."

We sat on the upholstered bench. I don't suppose we waited long, but evidently I had had enough for the moment, because I fell asleep, and was woken by Mr. Small saying: "I should think they'll be having us in any moment now. Another gentleman and Mr. Watts have just gone in."

The secretary with the friendly voice came out of her little office. "Mr. Gillett will see you now," she announced. We went through two doors, and entered the office. Mr. Watts carried out the introductions. There was a third man there, who spoke pleasantly when he was introduced, but said nothing throughout the interview.

This time there were no disbelieving comments and no pompous attempts to impress. I felt there was a genuine desire to see if I

could be fitted in somewhere, and to find out what were real possibilities. They were interested when I produced the Braille frame and
showed appreciative amusement at the cheque template. Mr. Gillett
was sympathetically concerned when I talked about getting around
on my own. "There are a lot of noisy trolleys in this place, and it
could be dangerous," he remarked. When the interview was over,
he said: "You could do with some tea before you set off back, I
expect. And I'll get a car to run you back to the station."

There were two other visitors having tea, and we all squashed into
the car together, so that Mr. Small had no chance to say anything
until we got out at the station. "I reckon we're all right," he commented then. "I fancy they'll be offering you a job."

He wanted to return to London that night, and I said I should be
able to get back to Church Stretton on my own. I had done it before,
and the only problem likely to arise was the change at Shrewsbury.
As my train pulled out, I thought of the last trip I had made on my
own.

V.E. Day had come. The war in Europe was over. The church bells
rang in Stretton with such clamour that I lost my bearings, and had
to ask my way. They were joyous bells, signalling victory, and not
the invasion under whose threatened shadow Britain had lain for
so long. The lights were going on again, too. Before my blindness
I had looked forward to seeing them go on—but now the spectacle
would have to be imagined.

Padre Nugee, temporarily acting as Commandant of the Training
Centre, announced that there would be a few days' holiday to mark
the victory. There would be festivities, but getting men to their
homes and back would be too big an operation to mount. When I
said I thought this was an occasion to celebrate with one's family if
one could, he replied that was up to me, but no arrangements would
be made by the organisation. After nearly five years under discipline
it was still quite hard for me to appreciate that I was a free agent,
and could go where I pleased—so long as I could manage the
mechanics of going. I said that if that were the case I would be
heading north.

I called in at the railway station to ask about trains, telephoned home to tell Margaret to expect me the next day, and worked out my route. I could arrange an early breakfast and walk the mile or so to the station. That would be easy enough, but I hoped it wouldn't be raining. I should need a porter or the help of a friendly stranger at Shrewsbury to change trains, and in Manchester I should have to get a taxi to the bus station. The bus passed my door, although there was no official putting-down point in the area. Still, with a bit of luck the driver might be prepared to make an unofficial stop. This was the way it had worked out when I had gone from Church Stretton to Burnley.

So I remembered that successful journey after V.E. Day, and saw no reason why the journey back to Church Stretton from Birmingham shouldn't work out as easily. Actually, it was even easier. The compartment filled up, and two of the passengers turned out to be W.A.A.F.s, who were also changing at Shrewsbury and going on to Ludlow. There was even a car waiting to meet me at the station. I felt that it had been a good day and that the portents augured well.

My hopes were justified. Soon afterwards a letter arrived from Cadbury Brothers offering me employment as a member of the clerical staff. I accepted with alacrity, and started on an extensive course of reading to try to fit myself for such opportunities as might offer themselves. With the help of readers I studied the publications of the Institute of Personnel Management, the Industrial Welfare Society, etc., and also the literature sent to me from Bournville, in particular one or two copies of the Bournville Works Magazine and the Cadbury publication *A World-Wide Business*. I had no previous experience of industry, and had not even gone beyond visiting one or two factories, but was quite excited at the prospect of trying my hand in this new field.

I applied my mind to increasing my competence in coping with everyday life. One of the most important problems was likely to be the "simple matter" of getting about safely on my own in a city I had never seen and didn't know. The mobile St. Dunstaners in Church Stretton generally walked in the road with the kerb as the guide line; but this would obviously be unsafe in a busy city, especially as traffic increased with the end of wartime restrictions.

I decided to spend more time acquiring the technique of walking on pavements. There would be more obstacles, and on occasions I might have to walk with my stick out in front of me, even though I felt acutely self-conscious when doing so; for I was still labouring under the notion, which I now consider quite mistaken, that I should try to walk as much like a sighted person as possible.

I have mentioned the difficulty I found with kerbs, which caused three types of injury: stubbing the toe against an up kerb I failed to notice in time; jarring the spine when stepping flat-footed off a surprise down kerb; and catching the ankle on the edge of a kerb if I slipped off or misjudged the step. By listening for the sound changes as I approached the end of buildings, I found a way of at least knowing when to expect the end of a street, so that I could slide my stick to look for the kerb edge. I profited, too, from the habit acquired in the gymnasium of pointing the toes when stepping or jumping down; this meant the step down off a kerb was cushioned by the ball of the foot and the "give" of the joints.

I was not content to walk slowly, and decided I should just have to risk meeting unexpected obstacles (until my obstacle sense was further developed) as part of the blind man's "cross". I had read of a blind man whose sight was restored when he walked into a lamp-post; it was an ironical thought that no amount of lamp-post encounters would do that for me. There was the redeeming feature, of course, that once you had met a lamp-post unexpectedly and forcibly, you knew where it was and remembered.

I kept up my daily period of handwriting and typing practice. Writing was quite easy by now, except for the care needed to ensure there was no overwriting. I tried hard to think of ways of avoiding this. The apparatus available seemed clumsy, and the only solution that occurred to me was to keep the index finger of my left hand at the beginning of a line, spacing my words out well along the line, and then to move the finger down to mark the start of the next line, allowing rather generous space between lines.

Then there was the old problem of finding out which way round your nib was, without getting your fingers dirty. I was delighted when Sir Ian Fraser showed me the prototype of a new ball-point pen which the Miles Company was developing. I thought the flow of ink produced by such a pen would make for handwriting that looked rather spidery, but this would be far outweighed by its obvious advantages. It was a great joy some months later to receive one of these pens through St. Dunstan's.

There was a popular song of the time which we adopted at Church Stretton as a sort of theme song: "Oh, give me land, lots of land, And the heavenly sky above, Don't fence me in." It helped to dispel the shut-in feeling we all had now and then. Indeed the whole period at Church Stretton was punctuated by times of heavy stress, even of despair; but they were outweighed, for me anyhow, by the genuine camaraderie I found there, some very close friendships formed, and contact with some remarkable people, both sighted and blind. I still remember the blackest moments—they burned too deep for the scars ever to heal completely; but the overall impression remains one of fun and happiness, and of real progress towards rehabilitation, although the crucial tests were still to come. Church Stretton was only a "transit" camp, but a transit camp where I was very content to be.

Perhaps it was the desire to be going forward to the next stage which has blotted out my memory of the last days there. The daily round based on Brockhurst was suddenly over, and all at once I was at home preparing for the move to Birmingham. In between our preparations we spent a few days at Huddersfield with the newly-weds, Ted and Marjorie Barton. It was the first of many visits we have exchanged, but it is the one I remember most vividly.

Although at Church Stretton we had jokingly described ourselves as "psychological cases", I am sure we should not have been so amused if people had taken the remark seriously. A hint of the real state of things came to me as I stood in the Bartons' garden one morning. Margaret had gone shopping in the village, and I suddenly had a panic-stricken feeling that she would not be coming back. It was a fear utterly irrational and without foundation but reflected, I think, some of the tensions I had been labouring under during the past twelve months. I shook off the fear, but even so was much relieved when she returned with her purchases.

I was impressed by the new garden path Ted had laid. I felt it would not have occurred to me to undertake such a task, and profited from the object lesson. I profited, too, from the opportunity of applying the technique I was developing for learning a new environment, particularly a different house. This consisted of noting any distinctive characteristics which marked the entrance, and the areas immediately short of and beyond it. The next point to note was the relative position of the entrance and the front door, its characteristics, and those of the surface leading to it. This information would give me a reasonable chance of finding the right house again, if I chose to go out alone.

Inside a house that was new to me, once I had been given an idea of the general lay-out, and any special perils such as fragile family heirlooms, I much preferred to be allowed to explore a room completely on my own; it was very embarrassing to go round it with my hands in others' presence. But a quick survey on my own gave me a much more vivid and thorough knowledge of the room. This was not usually possible, however, and where I couldn't make my survey, I kept a mental check while in the room, using my ears to note the position of doors, a fire or clock, and any other features.

Sounds outside often told me where there were windows, and they could also give a valuable clue to the room's position in relation to the area outside the house; also the position of roads, a farm, or anything else nearby which had distinguishing sound clues. Knowing the time of day, and sunlight coming into a room, gave a compass bearing which helped to make the picture a little more precise.

This was a help, too, towards establishing my bearings in a house with turns in corridors or stairs. The use of handrails, besides being a sensible safety precaution, provided a good deal of valuable information about the nature of the building; and for various reasons it was helpful to observe the type and position of door-knobs or handles—although often I couldn't find this out because people rushed to open the door for me!

Each morning at the Bartons' we walked through the fields to the neighbouring farm to collect the milk, and we must have looked like a parody of "Lead, kindly Light" as we returned—with Ted in front carrying the milk can, and me behind. We hardly ever walked side by side, as Ted preferred to walk in the road, because his hearing had been damaged and he had no obstacle sense, while I was for staying on the footpath. I still get a twinge recalling one incident connected with this. I thought I knew where the lamp-posts were, and was walking along the footpath trying to keep pace with Ted who was stepping it out on the road, following the kerb. I walked head on into a lamp-post, catching it fair and square in the middle of my forehead. I knew what sort of comments Ted would make about the dangers of walking on footpaths if I said anything, so I just had to take it in silence.

Lower down, the lane ran into a main road, the kerb following a broad sweep. I thought we had gone right round and were making the shortest possible crossing; but when we had done about thirty paces and were still apparently in the middle of the road, I told myself one ought to be much more careful in deciding the angle to cross a road at, whether the road was wide or narrow. There was little traffic in those days of petrol rationing, but two cars actually came along to reinforce the lesson.

Ted seemed to be making progress in his job as a chemical engineer. I felt he was indeed lucky to have a man assigned to him to help him with his calculations. I wished I had had some sort of technical qualification instead of the purely academic knowledge my years of study yielded. This was not quite a fair assessment, I realise now, but at the time I couldn't see how I could apply anything I had studied to industry.

The next day the explosion of the first atomic bomb in the Pacific ruled out all other possible topics of conversation. It was something so incredible in its implications that the mind boggled. Our world was indeed going to be a very different place.

A one-day visit to Birmingham to try to find accommodation proved futile. It did, however, establish that an old friend of mine, Ken Bannister, a lecturer at Birmingham University, was living within a couple of miles of the Bournville factory, where I was due to start work very shortly. I had not seen Ken since the beginning of the war, but felt sure that he would be ready to help if he possibly could. I telephoned him and he said of course we must stay with them for a week or two until we could find something suitable. It was a most friendly act, because he was at the time absorbed in technical research, and Mary Bannister was about to have her third child.

The day came to leave the town which had been home to us for so long. Margaret rather felt we were going to the ends of the earth. To me it was another move, "fresh woods and pastures new", and the opportunity for a new life. It seemed as though the neighbourhood shared my wife's feelings, because they all turned out to see us off and wish us well.

# CHAPTER 8

## FINDING AN OPENING

Our first big problem was to find accommodation. Birmingham had a serious housing shortage even before the war, and this was aggravated by the destruction of thousands of houses during the air raids. After the war, to make matters worse, thriving industry brought in a flow of new population. The arrangement with the Bannisters was of course only a stop-gap, and Margaret spent miserable days pushing the pram round the area in search of somewhere to live. We appealed to St. Dunstan's for help, but the member of their housing department who visited us did not appear able to do much for us.

Finally I appealed to Mr. Charles Gillett, who immediately understood the position and said he would see to it that one of the houses belonging to Cadbury Brothers was made available to us for renting. He also suggested places in the area where the house must be situated if I was to get to work easily. I should perhaps say here that in the course of a long association since then I never went to see Mr. Gillett without coming away cheered by his unfailing good humour.

Then Bert Johnson, one of the senior engineers responsible for overseeing the firm's property, visited me in the office where I was trying to fill my time; and this visit, too, was a big boost to my declining morale. He also made it his business to get our housing problem solved, but besides that showed that he realised what it must be like for a blind man trying to fit himself into a new job. He had various sensible ideas for me, and—unlike the person whose office I had been put into—was quite ready to believe there were lots of things I could usefully do.

Mr. Tatham, the director who had remained completely silent throughout my selection interview, also called in to see me. He announced his name, and was quite impressed when I said: "Ah yes, you were present at the interview I had with Mr. Gillett."

I remarked that I should have been a bit lacking in ordinary *savoir-faire* if I hadn't made a point of remembering the people who had interviewed me. Among other things, he commented on the cheque template which I had produced at the interview. It was clear that it had helped to swing things in my favour; and I felt rather glad, in spite of the difficulties I was meeting, that I had not produced it at my interview in Blackpool.

Bert Johnson did not waste time. He arranged to meet Margaret, and before very long it was settled that we should move into the house where we still live.

We had discovered a friend, Lesley Smith, living in a block of flats for business women quite near the factory; I had known her brother, who had been killed doing experimental flying with aerial torpedoes in the Fleet Air Arm, and also knew her fiancé. While Margaret returned to Burnley to arrange for the removal of our furniture, I was housed in the Visitor's Flat, an event which was extremely unusual, if not unique. The stay was significant, because it led to my forming lasting friendships with two of the residents, Phyllis Muscott and "Henny", as Miss Henderson was known to all her intimates.

We were delighted with the house once we had moved into it. On several occasions I was on the point of deciding that there was no future for me at Bournville, but was restrained from drastic action because we found our living conditions pleasant. It is important to have good neighbours if you live in a semi-detached house, and we were favoured in this respect too.

As far as work went, I was at first placed in the Works' Council office, where I soon discovered that Bournville had for over twenty-five years been doing the things Walpole had written about in *Management and Men*. There was already an elaborate organisation, in which everybody concerned seemed to be fully occupied, and I couldn't see any opening.

At my request St. Dunstan's had had a Braille copy made of the firm's internal telephone directory; I studied this, learning any numbers that might be useful, and also the list of members of the senior management staff and their departments. It seemed from the latter that the best openings were likely to be on the sales or advertising side, but I couldn't think of anything I could do in that connection. There was little need to advertise or try to sell chocolate. Rationing was to stay with us for some years and people would take all the chocolate they were allowed to have.

I found a few people who could spare a little time to tell me something of the organisation. I knew already that there was a wide range of leisure activities employees took part in, many of them through independent works' societies, which had a minimum of organisational help from the Works' Council Office. If I couldn't find any work to do during the day, might there not be opportunities in the evenings? The B.B.C. was putting on a series of programmes designed to stimulate discussions on the resumption of family life after the upsets and vicissitudes of the war. I got support for my suggestion that it might be useful to try to form such a discussion group at Bournville. I formed a group, which only managed to keep going for a few weeks, but at least I had actually done something.

Out of sheer kindness of heart, a member of the Planning Office staff, Frank Fielding, had taken on himself the role of escort during the mid-day break. There was a very big Dining Block, where 2,000 people could dine at once, and adjoining it were playing fields and two swimming pools. They made an extensive area which at first seemed rather bewildering, but the mid-day strolls we took soon brought me enough familiarity with it to get about alone when I wished.

Mr. Gillett was concerned that there seemed to be no openings for me in the Works' Council office. He followed a well-established practice by which the director who included responsibility for boys within his sphere had an annual interview with every youth under eighteen. Matters requiring follow-up often arose from these interviews. This was done by "Eddy" Edmundson, secretary of the Bournville Youths' Club, an organisation which provided social and leisure facilities for male employees under twenty-one. Mr. Gillett thought I could help with this follow-up work, which mainly took the form of further interviews. In this way I was brought into contact with the youths of Bournville, and at once I saw possibilities. I had taught in a boys' school. I had had responsibilities for young men in the Air Force. Dealing with youths and young men was something I knew about. I must cast around for something not being done, which could be regarded as useful, and do it. I had been reared in the doctrine of "God helps those who help themselves".

In the follow-up interviews I was conducting, the aim was often to suggest courses of study or leisure activities which might help forward the youth's progress. Although there were two swimming baths within the Bournville factory area, life-saving training for youths was not one of the leisure activities promoted at that time. Training boys to take the examinations of the Royal Life Saving Society had been one of my extraneous activities as a schoolmaster, so I asked myself, "Why not try to start life-saving as an activity in the Youths' Club?"

At first thought the difficulties appeared considerable. It was eight years since I had done any such training, and I should need to study the handbook again. I could carry out the instruction on land, because I could easily check whether instructions were being followed, but what about in the water? And suppose there was an accident and somebody got into serious difficulties, or even drowned? After thinking over the difficulties and risks, I decided there were ways round them, and I needn't be deterred from such an attempt so long as I made sure the necessary safeguards were observed. While I was considering these possibilities, I was at last given a real assignment.

Mr. Gillett was adult chairman of the Bournville Works Youths' Committee, an experiment in junior joint consultation which had been set up in 1920. It was a committee consisting of elected youths' representatives and adults nominated by the board of directors, and was concerned with the well-being of males under twenty-one employed at Bournville. Food was rationed, and the factory was allowed to buy food on a scale related to the total number of employees and the number of meals served. The committee had expressed concern that the junior male employees were not getting their proper ration because they tended to make do with things like cakes and mineral waters. I was asked to conduct a survey and make recommendations, and was told I could get a limited amount of sighted clerical help from the Women's Council Office; generally this was provided by an attractive, auburn-haired junior, named Corris.

Things were looking up. The survey would not take long, but I could profit by the help made available to pursue my other idea. I conducted the survey by going into the youths' club premises at mid-day, putting questions to a lot of ready volunteers; and found that the impressions which had existed were substantiated by the facts. I proposed that a system should be introduced of providing a set meal at a subsidised price, and recommended that this should be sixpence for youths aged fourteen, a shilling for those above that age. The Board accepted the proposal, but set the price at ninepence for all youths. I felt slightly snubbed, but had clearly not committed any major gaffe.

Meanwhile I had refreshed my knowledge of the handbook of the Royal Life Saving Society, and made some useful Braille notes. I had also discovered some youths who were interested in receiving life-saving instruction. I started off, and found that my ideas worked out in practice. In the land-training, demonstration and verbal explanation, supplemented by a quick manual check, proved quite adequate. The sound of the drill being performed gave me a reliable idea of how it was being done. The object of this land drill was to ensure that the actions needed in the water were carried out automatically; I could use one of the members of the group to check for me that this was happening. Those acting as subjects soon told me if their rescuer had not carried out the "rescue" satisfactorily.

It was certainly not what I had thought of doing in industry, but it was something. I had decided I was prepared to try my hand at anything, however insignificant it might appear, so long as it gave me a chance of showing there were things a blind man could do. I remembered something Mr. Small had said during my Bournville interview. He had been asked in general terms what sort of jobs blind men were doing. He mentioned some of them, and then went on: "Of course, the higher up he gets, the less his lack of sight matters, because he can use others' sight. With all due respect, you gentlemen are often in the same situation as a blind man when you study reports on which you have to make decisions. In the same way, you no doubt often arrange for others to transport you from place to place."

The adult discussion group I tried to set up had feebly petered out, but a junior group, based on the B.B.C. series, "To Start You Talking", had been extremely well supported, and was regarded by the local B.B.C. Education Officer as one of the liveliest groups of the kind in the country. Although the kind of work I had thought of doing was not available, there were apparently other opportunities if I could seize them, or even create them. Fred Beech, a senior foreman who had attended both the adult and junior discussion groups, gave me the friendly tip that Mr. Gillett was considering the idea of my transfer full-time to the youth side. I was sure I could contribute something worthwhile in that field, but it would be essential to have some sort of status. This time I would have to know what I wanted, and be prepared to ask for it.

I reflected on moments in the past when opportunity had seemed to be in the air, but modesty, shyness or reticence had caused me to let the moment slip. "There is a tide in the affairs of men," I ruminated—but this wasn't a question of fame or fortune; it was a straightforward issue of survival as an employee on the Bournville pay-roll. I wasn't so utterly ignorant as I had been when I arrived a few months before. I didn't need to sit around waiting for somebody who wasn't interested to try to put one or two makeshift bits of work in my way.

Admittedly, however, the operations of the Youths' Committee were very limited, more or less confined to the holding of a monthly meeting and the production of minutes; I had attended the meetings when doing the meals survey. With my knowledge of Braille and ability to type, it would be easy for me to produce minutes. If this transfer were offered, I would accept with alacrity, and ask to be made secretary of the Youths' Committee.

Probably Mr. Gillett had already had the same idea. When he and Mr. Tatham saw me again, I made my request, and they promptly agreed. I was very much encouraged by the line they took at this interview, which I felt marked a decisive stage in my career. At least the situation now looked distinctly promising. For I knew there were worthwhile things I could do if given an opportunity; and now I had been given one.

CHAPTER 9

BOURNVILLE

It seemed a significant moment for me and my family, and as often on such occasions I did a bit of private stock-taking. In hospital, at Church Stretton and at Bournville, I had found all too much time for reflection. I remembered telling my friends when it became clear that war was inevitable: "I don't mind the thought of being killed, but I hope to God I'm not mutilated and left to drag out my life as a burden to others." When Neville Chamberlain made his broadcast declaring war on Germany, I slipped out of church between reading the two lessons to hear the broadcast in a nearby house, and whispered the news to the vicar as I took my place at the lectern. I went to Blackburn next day to volunteer for the Navy—as it happened, they wouldn't take me; but my "war" assumed a very different pattern from the one I had expected. It seemed ironical to have sustained what many regard as the worst disability, without having ever been a combatant.

As a choirboy I had sung "Oh death, where is thy sting, Oh grave, where is thy victory?" so often that philosophical acceptance of death seemed quite normal. To accept life was often a more difficult problem.

I had no need to ask: "Oh life, where is thy sting?" The sting was there all round me: the baby daughter I couldn't see, in whose presence I had to take care lest I should do an irreparable injury; the simple things I couldn't do that a child could do so easily; all the things I had so enjoyed doing which I could never do again; the frustration I felt when people said: "If you could see, you'd understand what we're talking about"; the stupidity of those who thought because I was blind I was also deaf and mentally defective; the beauties of colour and form I should never again experience; the way people preoccupied with their own affairs would by-pass me as they wouldn't dream of doing with a sighted person; the forced dependence on others in so many things; and the realisation that whatever I did, I could never escape this dependence.

Such were my thoughts in black moods. Once I was so depressed by my chances of a future at Bournville that I went up to London to ask Sir Ian Fraser about other ideas for work. He was very reassuring, but I did not really believe what he said, although I took his advice to stay put. The same advice came to me in regular letters from two friends, one Margaret's godfather, the other the St. Dunstan's supporter who had "Brailled" for me the 1944 Education Act: they kept admonishing me to be patient and peg away steadily, against the day when someone would say: "He could do that job."

Their encouragement was one of the many credit items, which made me hope, despite all the debits, that I could eventually declare a dividend. An even larger credit item, of course, was Margaret's unwavering loyalty, bearing as she did the harder role of emotionally involved onlooker. Other blokes, sighted and blind, had not had the same good fortune with their marriages. My baby daughter was healthy and normal. To provide for these two, I had all the incentive I needed. My mind was clear, my hearing normal, my constitution unimpaired.

If I had got that Ministry of Pensions job, I might never have converted officialdom to the idea that a blind man should be treated just like anyone else, and given the same opportunities and rewards, provided he makes the grade. Here at Bournville they were obviously concerned with people as people, and there was a noticeable absence of "kowtowing". At the first interview with the two directors, I had been extremely interested to note the employment manager's relationship with them. There was no impression of subordination; his function was to help them reach the right decision, and he was clearly respected as the possessor of an independent mind. At Bournville the top management were looking for talent, you could feel, and were ready to recognise it. If I had talents which could be used in the organisation, there would be no faint-hearted restrictions or red-tape restraint.

I felt very happy telling Margaret the news of my transfer, and my new position as secretary of the youths' committee. I had a *raison d'être*, even if so far there was little enough to the job; but it was for me to make it into something more.

I weighed up the advantages and disadvantages of my situation. This was a field in which I had no previous experience, in a city I did not know, among people I did not know, and who did not know me. There were certain basic difficulties in the way of obtaining information. I could not read letters or study reports, documents or books without sighted help, and there was only a minimum of that available. Most of the geography of this large enterprise, employing some 10,000 people within the one complex, was entirely unknown to me. There were many dangers to be guarded against in exploring it. It seemed a pity that radar or asdic couldn't be used to help blind blokes like me to get around. It seemed an even greater pity, with fantastic achievements like splitting the atom, that the scientists hadn't got round to inventing a machine that would read.

Communication in the other direction was no difficulty. Having learned to type by touch, I could write more quickly and legibly than I had been able to do in my sighted days. With the help of Braille and the numbers I had memorised, the telephone was a quicker way of contacting many people than trekking round the factory to call on them. Braille or the dictaphone could be used for preparing reports or anything else which needed revision before being produced in its final form. I could learn people's voices instead of recognising their faces. My disability had the advantage that once seen my face was likely to be remembered. In hospital I had regretted that my right eye socket had been stitched up, and that the left eyelid had lost its use. These unusual features might have something to be said for them.

About this time I read an account of some research into employing the blind: the main conclusions were that the possible field was much wider than many were prepared to recognise, given a sympathetic environment and adequate training or experience. I had had no training in this field, but I felt I had had a good deal of valuable experience; what I had been through had increased my understanding of life and human beings. The environment here was certainly sympathetic, and altogether I was surely one of the totally blind who could be usefully employed!

By its terms of reference the youths' committee was directly responsible through its chairman (then Mr. Gillett) to Bournville's board of directors for the well-being of junior male employees. A great deal was done for these boys and young men, but there was nobody who knew them all personally. I felt if I got to know as many of them as possible individually, it would be a useful contribution in a big company like Cadbury's. I would try to gain their confidence and respect, possibly even their friendship. In the unsettled conditions after the war, when a generation of youngsters had missed the disciplining influence of fathers and male school-teachers, youths in industry presented a good many problems. I was someone with time to spend on helping to solve such problems.

I had to devise ways of getting to know the young recruits to industry in a natural and "incidental" manner. The contact had to be personal, and in this respect a blind person worked under obvious limitations. But I found I had compensating advantages: I could not register a face, smile across a room at someone or nod recognition; I had to talk to people to get to know them, and to talk to them often in order to remember voices and their owners. So I had to do things together with the youths I was concerned with. I could take part in formal interviews, and keep classified Braille and typed notes as aids to memory; but I had also to find activities I could effectively join in.

This meant taking more and more part in the club's life, which accordingly involved a good deal of evening work. I found I was also being kept busy in the day, so that I was doing a sixty-hour week. As usual Margaret made no complaint at having to spend long evenings alone at home.

At the first youths' committee meeting where I acted as secretary, I was embarrassed by the noise of my shorthand machine, but nobody else seemed to mind. I found, as I had expected, that I had no difficulty with the minutes, but I made a practice of typing out the draft immediately after the meeting. I had been advised to use

Braille as little as possible, and this advice proved sound. I had the shorthand machine on my desk, always ready, so that I could make any memo notes I needed. I kept some Braille notes about the youths I was specially concerned with. These could be extremely confidential without danger of their being read by others, as there was nobody else around with a knowledge of Braille.

I also used Braille for notes of talks I had to give, reports to present, or memoranda to be prepared. The Braille pocket frame was most useful for making notes I wished to read myself, but I found it too slow for the many small notes about minor things to be done which I could not risk forgetting. To solve this need to make quick notes, I started writing in longhand on the cards I carried for use with the Braille frame. One of the girls in the office would then read them back to me—if she could. This was often no easy matter, since the notes were written under all sorts of conditions. Normally I would write them standing, resting the card on my left hand, and then as a rule they were not too hard to read; but if they had been written on a bumpy bus ride, inspired guesswork might be needed, and the results were sometimes highly hilarious. Still, the system has worked with pretty fair success over the years.

Often a card would only carry one note on one side; so to avoid having to carry too many cards, I adopted a method of puncturing the card from the other side after I had written on it. This meant that there were raised dots along the edge of the card on the side I had written on. An urgent memo, which required prompt action and therefore must be read, would carry a line of several dots. Other notes, not so urgent, would be indicated by one or two dots. If I came to the end of my supply of cards, I could use the opposite side of cards I had already written on. Cards bearing messages were always placed in my left-hand pocket, so that a card in that pocket meant something on which action was to be taken. I also used this pocket for money which had to be paid in to the club cashier. This system eased the load on my memory, which was being taxed more and more every day.

At the end of my first full year at Bournville I was given an encouraging rise in salary. At the end of the following year I was

promoted to the junior management staff, and two years after that
to the senior management staff. Seen in retrospect, this was quick
advancement. It represented the complete confidence shown in me
throughout by Mr. Gillett, who was my director and who had
appointed me originally. I like to think it also showed the Board
was satisfied with the contribution I was making to Bournville.

It was obvious from the start that nobody had any clear idea what
I would be able to do, or should be asked to do. When I was transferred to the youth side, it was also made clear that I would be
given considerable freedom to work out for myself the directions
in which I could be usefully engaged. I had been immediately impressed by the very broad view Cadbury Brothers took of their
responsibilities as employers. I discovered they had been doing more
advanced things on the labour relations side than I had learned
about in my sketchy reading. For instance, every employee under
eighteen was given one day off per week, with pay, to pursue a
course of non-vocational education at the Bournville Day Continuation College. The youths' club provided a wide range of opportunities for enjoyable leisure activities. It was also the link for
maintaining contact with men away in the forces, old club members,
who visited the club in impressive numbers when they came back
on leave or for good.

Most of the foremen in the various departments took a personal
interest in the youths under their control, but as I have said, nobody
knew them all; I meant to work towards doing just that. A large
organisation is almost bound to become impersonal in some ways,
and I hoped I could take some of the impersonality out of it. With
the right sort of liaison, the right guidance given at the crucial
moment, difficulties could be forestalled. In the post-war period of
separations and broken homes, there were many youths with
particular troubles: they might respond to genuine interest from a
person with time to spare. Some of the work would be of a stop-gap
"first-aid" nature, but some could be thought of as real training for
life and industry, helping to shape character and produce men who
would continue the traditions of a firm with a fine reputation. This
idea was the foundation of what I meant to do. It still is.

Towards my objective of getting to know as many of "my" youths as possible, I arranged to interview every boy as soon as he joined the firm (this could be fitted conveniently into the usual three-day induction course), and afterwards to interview them every year. I supplemented my knowledge by many extra contacts, as for instance at the annual fortnight's summer camp—where I ran the camp shop—and by selling things at the club canteen. It was part of my routine to be around the factory club premises at mid-day every working day.

A few simple ideas have governed my dealings with the youths for whose welfare I was responsible to the Board. Somehow I must gain their confidence. Generally I could do this by convincing them that I was really on their side. I must find forms of worthwhile activity they could become involved in, following where possible the line of their own interests or abilities. One of the tenets of the Quakers is to seek "that of God in everyone"; and my disability is one which almost unfailingly brings out the best in people. This was a useful start for appealing to the idealism inherent in youth.

A youngster will generally respond to ideas which give him a sense of being thought well of, and considered a responsible person. You can't expect people to behave responsibly, I have always believed, unless they feel they are carrying responsibility. So my standard practice with youths has been the reverse of "give a dog a bad name". This has been made much easier to follow because of the social service tradition in the Bournville Youths' Club. Some of the most unlikely individuals have benefited from the service they have been persuaded to give others worse placed than themselves. A youngster from a difficult home background has gained a new view of life by helping put on an entertainment for crippled children and orphans. The appreciation of old people with overgrown lawns which have been restored to order by a club motor-mowing team, has given a real boost to the morale of the youngsters concerned.

Through his special experience a blind person can develop an extra sensitivity in his relationships, and right from the start I found this extremely useful in my new assignment. People generally are much more practised in controlling their features than in controlling the slight inflections in the voice which give away so much. Appearances are notoriously deceptive—but can't deceive the blind. The folk wisdom which personifies Justice as blind has something in it!

My "extra sense" or sensitivity has usually proved reliable in deciding when youths have or have not been telling the truth; and, remarkably enough, I have rarely known a youth, when I asked his name, give a false one. Occasionally total strangers trying to gate-crash a club function have done so, but even then there has usually been something in the voice which has prompted me to ask one or two more questions, and these in turn have shown up the attempted deception.

One tends to remember successes rather than failures. There was Tony. I was told that he had got mixed up with a gang who were stealing lead. Basically he was decent and hard-working, but of limited intelligence. The only point of contact I could establish with him was in teaching him to read. I also persuaded him to make a regular habit of saving. By the time he could read the newspaper, he had saved over £100. He used most of it to buy a motor-bike, and got into trouble once for speeding, but that was the only time he came up against the law.

There was Malcolm, whose family had been moved to a new housing estate as part of a slum clearance programme. The local louts were making life difficult for them, particularly for his crippled sister. He was not big enough to deal with them, and his resentment made him start stealing, even breaking into local shops and schools. He was kept so busy with various activities in the club, one of which he took as his own special responsibility, that he had no spare time in which to get into trouble. He also found one or two friends who "persuaded" the louts to keep away, and so was diverted from the path which had seemed to lead inevitably to Borstal.

One of the conspicuous failures was Robert. He had come to work via an orphanage and a remand home. In spite of all our efforts he could not be persuaded that there was a place for him in normal society, and in the end he went back to the remand home.

We had a group of youths whose job was delivering the internal

H                                    111

post. They were a lively bunch of young rogues, whose chief problem was that they needed to be kept busy every minute of the day. At a time of very full employment, it was difficult to recruit boys for this work, so that Cadbury's had to make do with what was available. Somehow we got on to the idea of producing the *Post Boys' Journal*. It certainly occupied their leisure, and possibly some of the time when officially they were at work, but it did help to keep them out of mischief.

My life-saving instruction fizzled out without my managing to present a single group for examination. I was depressed by this failure, which could be ascribed to my own inadequacy as a blind instructor, and it was some years before I decided to have another shot, profiting by my mistakes.

Another piece of work I tried was taking classes at the day continuation college when they were short of staff. In the front row of the first class I took there was a deaf youth, which really made an impossible situation! Generally I managed to cope with the classes reasonably well, but I did not go on with it very long, and the experience confirmed me in the belief that I had been right not to return to teaching.

Meanwhile, however, there were other directions in which my efforts produced a rewarding response. Dramatics, music-listening and discussion groups thrived. I was getting to know my environment and the people who filled it. Through two pieces of social research I carried out—into the leisure habits of young people, and the amount of their pocket money spending—I could contribute to an enquiry Mr. Seebohm Rowntree was making, in the course of which he visited Bournville. I also did a follow-up enquiry into youths who had attended Outward Bound School courses as holders of scholarships given by Cadbury Brothers. Some people were not too pleased with the conclusions I drew, but I believe they may have been something Kurt Hahn took into account in his ideas for the further development of these schools.

My first year at Bournville was certainly a time in the main for getting my bearings. Still, I began to find a routine establishing itself, for there was plenty of detailed administration connected with organising and stimulating activities for the young. During my second year it occurred to me that the 100 men and women from Bournville who had been killed in the Second World War ought to be remembered in some other way than by merely inscribing extra names and dates on the existing memorials.

When I raised this at a meeting of the youths' committee, Mr. Gillett suggested that perhaps a Travel Scholarship might be established. I developed this idea into a plan which became known as the Youths' Committee's War Memorial Scheme. Club members should combine to raise a sum of money, which would be spent over a period of years on projects calculated to foster good relations between the young people of Bournville and those of other countries. The target was set at £2,000, and the Board offered to donate one pound, up to £1,000, for every pound raised.

The money was raised in twelve months, mainly by organising Saturday night dances. This was an admirable way of involving young people in the organisation, and the only difficulties we met were those produced by success. At first the numbers attending were about two hundred. Our committee of helpers steadily raised its sights to attract first three hundred, then four hundred, then six hundred, the maximum legally allowed. The difficulties arose when the "House Full" notices went up within an hour of opening. Careful organisation and stewarding were needed to prevent unauthorised entry to a room which had sixteen separate possible points of entry! Inside the hall, despite the large numbers, control was never a big problem, although occasional minor episodes made me glad I was able to get round the building quickly and unaided.

The war memorial scheme fund of £2,000 was finally established at the Bournville youths' club's summer camp of 1948. Mr. Gillett came over specially to hand me the cheque for £1,000 presented by the Board of Cadbury's. In the discussions on how the scheme should operate, Harold Watts, the employment manager who had been present at my appointment interview, said: "Let it run for eight years. By the end of that time we shall know whether there is any point in trying to continue it." In fact the scheme has run ever since, and its value has proved itself over the years. By promoting exchange visits, it has helped in the building of friendships between the young of many nationalities, has encouraged a spirit of tolerance and understanding, and has kept green the memory of those who died for their country.

My own horizons were greatly extended by the war, and I had learnt to appreciate the *camaraderie* of the forces; as an ex-serviceman I naturally took a great deal of interest in the situation created by the continuance of national service. I knew that many of the young men involved, particularly those serving in Germany, were faced by fierce and pressing temptations; and I wrote a booklet, which was published with cleverly drawn and amusing illustrations, to try to give them a positive attitude to their service, with all the opportunities it offered, instead of regarding it as a waste of time and interference in their lives.

I saw each youth near the time when he registered for national service, and tried to advise him, particularly if there seemed types of service likely to prove valuable to him on his return. I kept up a liaison with the Army recruiting officers, which they seemed to appreciate a great deal. When a youth went for his "medical" and interview, he took with him a letter I had prepared setting out the things he had done, though not saying anything about his character or the quality of his work at Bournville. The aim was to help him into the branch of service he was most suitable for, without spoiling his chances, of course, if he was put in a different branch. I believe the system was justified by the very small number of our men who got into serious trouble while on national service, and the high proportion, one in three, who gained promotion during it.

Towards the end of 1948, one or two people at Bournville were considering ways of celebrating the fiftieth anniversary of the girls' athletic club and the youths' club. There had been a proposal to hold a pageant, but I doubted if our young people would be very interested. I proposed instead to hold a birthday party with a difference. It would be a Festival of Youth. There would be hundreds of young people, from different countries, all taking part in a wide variety of athletic activities from archery to water polo. In the evening there would be an indoor show, "Focus on Sport", with demonstrations by top exponents, such as Olympic Scottish dancers and world international table-tennis champions, rounded off with a mammoth dance and fireworks display, of which the final set-piece would be a reproduction of the Festival badge.

When I proposed the idea, I had not really meant that if it were adopted I should be responsible for organising the Festival. But Miss Hatton, Mr. Gillett's secretary, who had impressed me with her friendly understanding when I came to Bournville for my appointment interview, gave me the tip that I might be asked to take this on. I thought about it, and wondered if I could do it.

I should have had no doubt about it in my sighted days, but now? Could I keep my finger on all the detailed arrangements which would be involved? Where would I start? How would I find all the voluntary help needed? Perhaps I had better decline the offer if it were made. But no, this was unthinkable. The fact that the offer was being considered meant that C. W. G. (Mr. Gillett) thought me capable of doing the job. If I had had to persuade *somebody else* that I thought I could do it, I wouldn't have hesitated; so why should I be hesitating now? It would mean a fantastic amount of work, but it would be fun. It would also strengthen the case I had been making to have a competent secretary entirely for my work.

The offer was made. I accepted on the spot. I also got my secretary, Helen Rhind, a woman with three sons, the youngest of whom had two more years to do at boarding school; she did a valiant job. Scores of helpers volunteered to serve on the one main committee and the fourteen sub-committees responsible for organising the different sections of the Festival; I sat on each of them as secretary. There were two plans for the Festival, one for fine weather and one for wet. For its complete success, however, it was essential that June 1st, 1950 should be a glorious day. Mrs. Rhind, a devout Catholic, assured me that she had sought the aid of Saint Scholastica in the matter. Being C. of E., I didn't know any saints whose intercession might be invoked, but I certainly did my share of praying for good weather.

During the last few days before the Festival, Margaret had to travel north because of the death of an aunt. It had suited me to have a few days alone, because no one would be bothering about how late I was working. On the eve of the Festival I returned home very late, booked a telephone alarm call for six a.m., and slept like a log until the telephone rang. The operator assured me that it was a beautiful morning, and likely to continue so. It was such a beautiful morning that I decided to walk the two miles to work, and left home just before seven.

During the day, apart from a few difficulties which were quickly resolved, the arrangements worked like clockwork, right to the final shower of coloured fire as the Festival emblem spluttered out, to synchronise with the playing of the national anthem over the amplification system. There was still a great deal of clearing-up to be done: many letters of thanks to be written, hired and borrowed equipment to be returned, the day continuation college re-converted from a girls' dormitory, the Rowheath camp for boy participants struck; and full results circulated to all who had taken part. The Festival had meant twelve months' solid work as concentrated as any year of my life had been. It was not an important affair, but to me its success mattered tremendously. It was a wonderful highlight to the year which had seen my promotion to senior management staff.

Some 2,000 young people had been entertained for the day. They had come from 100 firms in nine countries to take part in a dozen different activities. It had certainly been worth all the effort, and I was heartily glad I had cast off the first doubts as to whether I could tackle it. I thought back to the comments of a colleague, Harry Briggs, with whom I had become friendly at the camp four years before: "Don't worry. There'll come a time when you aren't looking for work any longer, but have more than you can really handle."

Since the Bournville youths' club was started in 1900, the annual summer camp had been a most popular feature of the club's programme. Starting in 1946 at Bembridge in the Isle of Wight, I attended ten of these camps. At first, living in an open field, without the usual aids to orientation, I felt completely lost. There were sounds, however, which quickly became established as direction pointers—the occasional car along the Sandown road, the bugles of the nearby Boys' Brigade camp, the clatter of activity around the kitchen, or noises from the hotel across the next field. The lay-out of the camp was orderly, and I soon memorised the pattern. At night, I even found that I was at an advantage, because my stick, held out in front of me, gave protection against the guy ropes and tent pegs which were potential snares for the other campers.

To start with, I felt very much of a passenger, since there did not seem to be many things I could do. I helped with some of the camp chores, and then decided to produce a camp magazine. The Campers' Chronicle became a souvenir magazine, made up of the news-sheets which I produced daily. It sought to cover all the features of camp life, and the active co-operation of many of the campers gave me the incidental contacts I wanted. As camp routine and geography became more familiar, I found other ways of making myself useful, so that I could feel satisfied with my contribution to the general enjoyment.

Towards the end of one of these camps John Sherman, our Works doctor, with whom I shared a tent, read to me a letter from Sir Ian Fraser. One of the medical journals was producing a book on disabilities. He had been approached to write an article on "Blindness", but he thought it was something I might like to try. The article had to be produced within a month, and I was just about to take two weeks' holiday, so that I had time to devote to writing it. Fortunately, an old school friend of mine, Ken Pilling, had recently come to work in Birmingham. He helped me by reading my draft and suggesting where alterations were needed; he later read the proof too. I was delighted when the article was accepted, and printed as the first in the book.

During the next year I wrote a little booklet on the Bournville Works Youths' Committee entitled Twenty Years of Junior Joint Consultation. Reading the proof, I was amused by a rather "Freudian" error on the part of the typesetter: "They discover that the committee does matter" came out as ". . . the committee does natter". The booklet told an unglamorous but worthwhile story; while for me personally it represented progress from the Church Stretton afternoon when I had fallen asleep on the lawn as Elizabeth Nugee read me Walpole's Management and Men. That book had given me ideas about a possible occupation, and although things had not worked out as I had expected, my attempt to write on an industrial subject was not so far removed from the approach I had when I started. Certainly I was working in a field where people were ready to welcome ideas and give you a chance of carrying them out.

Events had shown that there were ways round the limitations imposed by blindness. I would always have to work harder than my sighted colleagues to achieve the same results but I was achieving a technique which was economical in time and effort. Being unable to skim quickly through printed matter would continue to be frustrating, but friends and colleagues now knew items that would interest me, and brought them to my notice. The combination of Braille and longhand notes worked admirably for a classified index system, which kept me up to date on the matters I was dealing with.

I could organise help when I needed it for getting to new places, but generally managed alone although occasional bumps seemed inevitable. Still, I had discovered an ointment called "Indian Balm", which was extremely efficacious, so I carried this around in my brief-case to apply at once when necessary. I didn't mind too much so long as nobody saw me bump into things, but the acute embarrass-ment of being observed bumping was worse than the physical pain!

Eight years after my abortive attempt to establish life-saving as one of the activities of the Bournville youths' club, I thought I would try again. The first attempt had at least shown that a blind person could instruct people effectively in life-saving. I felt it had failed because my control hadn't been good enough and the training had been too drawn out, so that the interest of my young trainees had evaporated: this mistake must not be made again—I would go for quick results, until the section was established. I joined some of our members in the normal swimming sessions, and thus recruited some likely candidates. I produced concentrated notes of the theoretical knowledge they needed, in which they were given an oral examination; and turned the land drill into a quick-fire per-formance so that they had little time for the inevitable larking about of vigorous and high-spirited youths.

When I presented my first class of four for the bronze medal examination of the Royal Life Saving Society, Inspector Frank James of the Birmingham City Police declared himself well pleased with the standard attained. The big hurdle was over, and I now had four young men who could be trained to instruct their fellows. The section was established, and progressed steadily. One of that first group also had good reason to be glad of his training, because that summer he rescued a friend who got cramp while swimming in Lake Geneva.

The Royal Life Saving Society has a graded series of examinations and re-examinations at various levels of achievement. Candidates achieving the required standard receive medals, and bars to these medals on re-examination. There are competitions for trophies as a further stimulus towards maintaining interest and proficiency. Most of the trophies are awarded to organisations in certain classes, based on the total number of examination successes gained by each organisation during a calendar year.

This kind of incentive is much greater, alas, than the nobler idea of fitting yourself to give effective help to someone in need. The Society's motto is *Quemcunque miserum videris, hominem scias* (know that anyone you see in distress is a fellow human being). But the idea of universal brotherhood recommended is less exciting to young people than the hope of helping to win a trophy for their school or club.

Recognising that fact, I suggested the following year to the members of our newly formed life-saving section that we should go in for a trophy put up for competition by all men's clubs in the British Commonwealth affiliated to the Royal Life Saving Society. Since clubs have no idea how the others are faring, they are stimulated to keep up an all-out effort throughout the year. Our members responded to the challenge. The section won the trophy, and indeed repeated this triumph every time it entered the competition afterwards.

Much more important, a large number of our youths were trained to give effective help in emergency. Altogether I know of sixteen cases where they gave such help. One of our members was awarded a certificate for resuscitating a woman who had tried to gas herself. Rescues have been carried out in the sea, rivers, and swimming pools, and in several countries. These incidents have helped to establish a tradition and secure the sustained effort which this kind of training demands.

Anyone concerned with the welfare of young people is always looking for activities which help to shape character; and the life-saving training, being a form of social service, fitted well into this pattern. Many other opportunities for service have come up, among them helping to establish an adventure playground in a crowded part of the city; building and renovating premises for youth organisations; and the motor-mowing service mentioned earlier, whereby teams of our members have each year kept in trim the lawns of some ninety old people.

With the establishment of the war memorial scheme in 1948, I had tried to develop projects which would bring our young people in contact with their counterparts in Europe. The opportunities for them to take part in these projects were, of course, mainly restricted to holidays. Over the years the scheme has involved some thousands of young people. With some the connection has been purely administrative, but many have had an association on a personal basis leading to friendships in several countries. In 1948 I led a working party of our young employees at Fontenay-aux-Roses near Paris, which restored a site used by the Germans as an anti-aircraft gun position to its former use as a sports track. The working party went on afterwards to a holiday centre in the French Alps, while I returned to join our large summer camp in the Isle of Wight. The following year I repeated the formula with a party to build a swimming pool at Ommen in Holland. I organised an increasing number of holiday groups which made visits abroad. As Britain moved towards becoming "an affluent society", the number of youths attending the annual camp declined, and the number travelling abroad increased. I therefore had less reason to go to the camp, and switched over to taking one of the groups travelling abroad.

The demand for the abolition of national service built up as the years passed. My experience at Bournville had convinced me that the experience was beneficial for most of the young men who went into it properly prepared and determined to make the best of it. For many of our factory youths the life in the services had been their university; others had been given opportunities of carrying responsibility not possible in ordinary civilian life. It seemed to me a pity that the German example between the wars had thrown such discredit on the idea of giving the country's youth the chance to display its capacity for service; the country, and its young people, could have benefited from an arrangement under which young men and women gave a year's service which would be constructive and positive.

Since there was no likelihood of this happening, I wondered whether we could develop our scheme at Bournville to supplement the training programmes which already existed. Mr. Michael Cadbury, now director responsible for youth labour, supported the idea, and discussions with colleagues produced a plan which became known as the Youth Projects Scheme. It was a programme for which I maintained a close responsibility. All the youths of nineteen and twenty were invited to apply for a scholarship to carry out a project which would take them away from Bournville for some weeks or months. They were to put forward their own ideas as to the form the project should take. Scholarships would be awarded on the applicant's record, judged against his project and his suitability for it.

We hoped the projects would reproduce the most valuable elements of national service: widening of horizons, service to the community, coping with new situations, and sometimes the experience of communal living. The range of projects carried out since then has been extremely wide, from work camps building a pipe-line for an Italian village or redecorating the premises of a school for mentally handicapped children in Switzerland: to individual efforts which have often helped people to "find themselves"—like the young gardener who, knowing no French, spent a month helping with the wine harvest on a small French farm. He triumphed over all the difficulties and returned with a confidence and drive of which he had never shown any signs before. Another youth developed a new scale of values through helping to run a home in this country for spastic children. I help with the selection, advise, and do the general administration for the scheme. I find it a fascinating part of my varied routine at Bournville.

The guitar vogue suggested a new club activity: a guitar-playing class. I play this instrument myself, as well as the piano, the piano accordion and the harmonica. A few years earlier I had got together some club members to form a harmonica band, and joined them in club entertainments. Now the guitar also proved a useful common interest for a fair number of young people.

Many, too, went in for the Duke of Edinburgh's Award Scheme. The expedition part of it fitted in well with activities I had already developed for the club: canoeing and walking, based on a cottage called Ffynon Badarn in Merionethshire, an old sheep farm under the lee of Cader Idris.

This was distinctly a "find", for I had gone out with two colleagues, Timothy Cadbury and Alan Cowling, to look at Radgoid Hall, a derelict property belonging to the Forestry Commission. But it was much too large for our purpose and also too dilapidated, so we drove away feeling very disappointed. I urged the other two to look out for something else in the area which would make a base for our weekend walkers. Less than a mile down the bumpy track, they spotted Ffynon Badarn, which had to be reached by jumping or fording a trout stream. After their inspection Alan and Timothy returned to say the cottage was just what we wanted. There were discreet enquiries and negotiations, then we bought it with half an acre of land for £100. Successive groups of club members formed working parties which restored the farm to a desirable mountain base, served by a track in reasonable repair.

Two senior members of the club started the canoe-building and canoeing section. One of these, Ivan Gough, tried to canoe across the channel, but collapsed from sun-stroke. Luckily he had an escorting motor-boat which I had arranged through the Cadbury representative in Dover.

Five of the apprentices built single canoes to qualify for the gold badge in the hobbies section of the Duke of Edinburgh's Award Scheme. One of them, John Sayer, who had known Ivan, thought he too would like to have a try at canoeing across the channel. Four of his friends caught his enthusiasm, and approached me to see if the five of them could do a cross-channel paddle as their expedition test.

I discussed the idea with Sir John Hunt, who pointed out that the gold badge expedition test required participants to cover fifty miles over difficult water, and to camp out for three nights during the journey. Obviously, the need to wait for good weather for the channel crossing would make it almost impossible to satisfy these conditions. Clearly, too, it was going to be an extremely hazardous affair, unless many precautions were taken; but Mr. Charles Cadbury (who had succeeded Michael Cadbury as director responsible for youth labour) agreed that the group should be supported, and gave me the charge of seeing it was properly organised.

The canoeists and I formed an action committee. We would raise the necessary money by organising special events in the club. A training schedule was drawn up, which included circuit training in the gymnasium, long paddles on the water of the nearby canal, weekend visits to Weston-super-Mare to get sea-paddling experience, and the fifty-mile expedition test as one of the final stages of preparation. We asked advice from everyone we could find with relevant experience.

Dick Waterhouse of Deal, holder of the single-canoe cross-channel record, was particularly helpful. He advised us about the best times for crossing attempts, diet before and during the crossing, likely and unlikely hazards, safety drill, etc; and also recommended me to Jim Atkins of St. Margaret's Bay, escort for cross-channel swimming record-holders, who had also accompanied Dick when he achieved the record. The chief customs officer at Dover was equally helpful, and agreed to a procedure which meant that we could get away at very short notice should weather conditions suddenly appear favourable.

We made careful enquiries about the best lifejackets for our purpose, and agreed that each canoeist should also carry a whistle and signal rockets; the lifejackets should be painted so that they would be easily noticeable. Canoes would be fitted, of course, with buoyancy bags and baler, and capsizing techniques and recovery techniques were practised in the indoor baths.

There were some minor snags and troubles during the preparations, and one of the five youths proved a bit difficult. In fact the whole venture could have ended in disaster when on the first practice paddle in St. Margaret's Bay he went outside the bay and after five minutes had tipped into the water. He could not get back into his canoe because of the swell, but John Sayer stayed with him until he was picked up by the Walmer lifeboat. Nobody was any the worse for the experience, apart from the shock to my system—for during the general alarm one woman told me she had seen four canoeists drown.

Five days later all five safely carried out the crossing from St. Margaret's Bay to Ouissant in Normandy. I stood in the back of Jim Atkins's escorting motor-boat, keeping in touch with them by amplified megaphone. We were met on the beach by a representative of the French press, sent there by a news agency which predicted disaster, and evidently hoped the troubles of the first practice paddle would have been repeated. Jim took the canoes back and we stayed the night at a hotel in Ouissant.

As we returned on the boat from Calais, I had plenty to think about, especially that first practice paddle. Admittedly Jim Atkins had not suggested it was unwise when I told him on the Saturday morning that we planned going round the bay in the afternoon. But would I have let our chaps go out if I had been able to see the conditions for myself? Supposing the "witness" had been accurate with her story of four drowned: no doubt someone would have said, "Well, what do you expect if you let a blind man have such responsibilities?"

I thought of the way we had jointly planned every stage of the enterprise, had tried to reduce to a minimum any risks involved. Somehow it reflected my approach to all the things I had done since I was blinded, assessing the snags as far as I could before trying anything new, but knowing there would always be hazards I couldn't possibly foresee. And a blind man must be prepared to take risks, or he will scarcely avoid degeneration of spirit. Besides, the element of risk is part of the essence of sport, as with our canoeists.

There was one further factor: I had prayed for the success of the enterprise, "if it be Thy will". Some of my closest friends scoffed at my religious beliefs and my faith in the efficacy of prayer. I could once again tell them: "It may not be rational, but it works."

# CHAPTER 10

# THE COMMON TASK

At home, as well as at work, the words of the old hymn often came
back to me with a new significance:

> "The trivial round, the common task
> Will furnish all we ought to ask."

There were indeed enough common tasks in the trivial round,
which were simple enough for the sighted, to keep a blind man
constantly on the alert.

A year or so after we set up house in Birmingham, our son Andrew
was born. After this Margaret felt more than ever pulled in two
directions, attending to the children's needs and helping me with
the things I couldn't manage unaided. Obviously the children came
first, and this increased the incentive for me to find answers to my
daily problems. There were also things I could do in the home to
ease her burden, not as a regular routine but to give her a break sometimes or in an emergency.

Here the kinaesthetic sense showed its tremendous value and
efficiency, for instance in finishing the washing up after a big party.
I prefer to be left on my own with such a job, so that I am not
distracted by people talking; there is then less danger of an accident
because something has been moved an inch or two. I suppose one
reason why accidents often happen at home is because you tend to
relax your concentration there and think of other things. Once
again, blindness means you have to concentrate nearly all the time,
otherwise you can so easily knock things over and break them, chip
something fragile when putting it down, walk into a child; or walk
into the edge of a half-open door, bark your shins on a chair, even
fall down a flight of stairs.

For this reason you have to develop a way of life in which "safety drill" and constant functioning of the remaining senses are automatic, while avoiding as far as possible the "blindisms" which tend to put sighted people off. The process has compensations, for every day holds the possibility of discovering how to carry out a simple operation more easily or more effectively than the day before. Tidiness and system help greatly in making a blind person's life easier: they relieve the strain on the memory, and you are less often obliged to search for things, always a potential source of accident.

The first time I tried to mow the lawn at the back of my house, I tried to make sure of covering the whole lawn by using long clothes props to divide it into small areas. It is on a slope, which makes keeping straight harder. I experimented with various methods, always seeking the simplest solution. Finally I decided my easiest and most effective method was to go right round the edges twice, then go to and fro across the width, the lawn being shorter across than long. A small portable radio acted as a sound beacon to steer towards in the parts of the lawn where I found it hard to keep a straight course.

At table, when replacing my cup or glass, just as when putting down anything fragile or in washing up, I adopted a habit of first feeling with my finger the surface on which the article was to be deposited; in this way I avoided the risk of approaching it too vigorously. I realised that, in the kitchen, putting taller things (like jugs or milk bottles) against a wall surface meant less chance of knocking them over; and there was less chance of cutting or puncturing my fingers if we had knives and sharp instruments always placed pointing in the same direction.

In the home, as in industry, accidents to the hand are among the commonest types of accident. Painful experience taught me the wisdom of adopting a curled-finger or back-of-the-hand technique when using the hands to look for things, or to keep contact with a guiding surface like a wall. There is then much less risk of getting splinters up the nails, forcing back the fingers, or catching a finger in an aperture. Again, when approaching a child to pick it up, you have less fear of poking a finger into its eye.

Almost all the normal activities concerned with running a home should be within a blind person's capacity. Cooking probably relies less on sight than most of these activities, although the blind person has to be specially careful when dealing with things which may burn or scald. There are many devices available which can help, although I have not made use of them. I prefer to use a gas stove for such simple cooking as I do, because I can hear the gas burning and thus know it is functioning.

The whistling kettle will tell a blind person when water is boiling; but when making the morning or late-night tea, which seems to have come to be regarded as my prerogative, I do without such aids. If I start with an empty kettle I find it is easy enough to gauge the amount of water which runs into it by letting the water run for only a few seconds. The feel of the kettle's weight is another indication of the amount of water in it. I always use the same gas ring, so that (except during times of short supply) the amount of gas is constant, and the time the kettle will take to boil can be assessed accurately.

When preparing the cups and saucers I like to follow an ordered routine just as though carrying out a checking drill, like a machine-operator or a pilot checking before take-off. The routine is always likely to be thrown out because someone has left the milk or the sugar in a different place, but that is "one of those things". On occasions, always in the early morning, I have been known to make the morning tea and forget to put the tea in the pot; but the use of a tea strainer has at once provided a useful check and made the product more to my wife's taste. To warm the teapot before brewing the tea, I locate the handle of the kettle with my right hand so that I know precisely where the spout is, and hold the teapot in front of the spout for a few seconds as the water boils.

When pouring things into any container, I guard against possible error—and making a mess—by holding the container over something appropriate, for example the kitchen sink if I am pouring milk, tea or a squash drink. If pouring something in small quantity, which needs to be measured, such as whisky, gin or a liqueur, I hold the measure over a glass so as to avoid waste. When squirting soda water into a glass, I control the amount by gauging the glass's weight.

I have had my mishaps with corks when opening wine bottles, and always with the same friends, so that this has now become a standing joke. Still, it is really quite easy if you concentrate on the operation; the mishaps have always occurred through my talking at the same time. I never try to pour wine at table if we are entertaining friends; there are too many embarrassing possibilities.

When pouring milk into a teacup, or cordial into a glass, I gauge the amount to be poured by sound and by the "feel" of the container from which I am pouring.

On the comparatively few occasions when I have needed to deal with medicines, I have identified the bottles by affixing Braille labels. The dosage has usually been one teaspoonful. I have measured this by pouring into a teaspoon held over a cup to catch the overflow. I have then transferred the contents of the teaspoon to an egg cup, so that the medicine could be given to my patient without fear of spilling.

As the children grew older, I tried to relieve Margaret's burden by helping with such household chores as did not make too heavy demands on my patience and nervous energy—like chopping wood, laying fires, making the beds, laying the table, and using the vacuum cleaner. There you had to be careful not to get the lead caught in the cleaner's mouth, to listen for any strange sound which might mean something was likely to be sucked in and block the cleaner—and of course, not to bump into furniture. On the last point, I think I use the kinaesthetic sense rather than picturing the room in my mind. I have walked about the house so often that I can gauge the distance, say, of the dining-room table from the door, without conscious thought or trying to keep the picture of the dining-room lay-out in my mind. Dusting I rarely tackle, because it is such a laborious and tedious business dealing with so many separate items, compared with the effort required in dusting for a sighted person.

It was some years before I developed a way of trimming the privet hedges surrounding our garden, or the edges of the lawns. Using shears didn't do the job too well, and I found it awkward picking up the privet which had dropped as I used the shears. Eventually I solved the problem by using secateurs, which I could manage with my right hand, feeling with the left hand the part to be cut. As I became more proficient, I also became over-confident and cut my left thumb and forefinger rather badly, once again learning the hard way that a blind person can't afford to let his mind wander when he is doing things. I now wear an old pigskin glove on the left hand, which seems to give an adequate margin of protection.

Are there greater strains in a marriage if one of the partners is blind than if both are sighted? I don't think there are enough reliable statistics to generalise. A survey carried out in the United States in 1965 showed that the marriage break-up rate for the blind was three times the national average. On the other hand, my experience of men who married while at the St. Dunstan's Training Centre is that the very great majority of their marriages have been happy and enduring ones. The creation of a happy married life is, I would think, one of the highest achievements a blind person can seek. In the early years of my blindness, this was the touchstone against which Margaret and I measured our changed circumstances. Blindness has certainly limited the things I have been able to do with the children as they grew up, but it has also produced compensations; so I doubt if, in the final balance, anything has been lost on that score.

When very young children are about, you have to be immensely careful not to walk into them or damage them by a rash movement. Soon, however, they reach an age when, without appreciating what blindness means, they can actually guide you under controlled conditions. Catherine was quite remarkable: at the age of two she several times steered me to a seat in a café or restaurant, and tried to guard against my bumping into people or things. Andrew was a good deal older than this before he was prepared to take such a responsibility seriously, although he was admirable once he had realised what was involved.

Children love stories, and I suppose there is no reason why a blind person should not read stories in Braille to children. If his

Braille reading is not fluent enough, he could read the story first and then tell it. I did not find time to do either, but used the stories I remembered from my own childhood days, and others which I made up on the spot. I found this extremely hard work, but the children seemed to like them and didn't mind having them repeated. When Catherine was seven, she was very ill with measles, fortunately during one of my holidays. I spent hours telling her stories, and although it was exhausting, I was thrilled that it gave her such pleasure and helped her through the illness.

Playing games of the imagination was easier. The children and I would sit on the stairs, pretending we were in the diner on the train, or flying in an aeroplane. Giving the children pickaback rides, skipping, throwing balls into a netball goal ring, building motor-cars on the sands for the children to sit in, leap-frog, dominoes, chess, and card games, tearing paper shapes: these and others were games I could join in with the children. As they grew older, I could help them learn to read. I wrote short block-letter words on the cards I used for memo notes, and later typed easy sentences for them. On car journeys I would help pass the time by joining in games like, "I spy with my little eye, something beginning with . . ." —restricting the choice of objects to things in the car. Incidentally, it has always struck me as perfectly natural to use the word "see" and similar words and phrases, and I like others to do the same with me without feeling embarrassment.

We were very lucky to be allowed the use of a private swimming pool, and I devised a method of teaching swimming both to our children and several others. It was encouraging that our friends had confidence in me and entrusted me with their children's safety.

To start with, we played games in the shallow water. They would sit on my back while I pretended to be a submarine, walking along with my head below the water, blowing bubbles, or I would hold them under the shoulders, lifting them up and down—a game we called "Bouncy bounce". As confidence increased, we played other games, perhaps even jumping in together. After showing them how to do a "dog paddle", and letting them practise pulling on the water with their hands and arms, I would stand near the step, facing it, while the aspiring swimmer stood on my thighs, ready to push off and glide to the bank when I gave the word. Later on I would move a little further away, until the child found he was swimming. Once they had learned to keep afloat, I got them going on the crawl and breast stroke, using land and water drill. For the latter, I held their ankles lightly while they practised the leg movements. Since we were generally in the pool on our own, I always made sure that I had a sighted person with me.

There was one occasion when the four Thorntons had gone to the pool. Catherine was swimming in the deep end, Margaret was sitting on a bench on the side of the pool and I was standing in the shallow end waiting for Andrew to come to me. He had not yet learned to swim. Suddenly Margaret shouted out: "Walter, Andrew's in the water." I felt in front of me. There he was, standing bolt upright, with his head about three inches below the surface of the water. He had evidently thought I was aware of his presence and had stepped in without my realising it. The incident was a greater shock for Margaret and me than it was for him. We carried on with our games without his knowing that the one we had just played was unintentional, and could have been unfortunate.

Later still, we could share the fun of practising various dives from different heights, and criticising each other's performance. While there was a good deal I could not tell about the quality of a dive, such as the starting stance, and flight through the air, I could gain a good general idea of the quality of performance by the sound of the entry; an awkward entry with its untidy sounds was very easy to recognise. The double sound of first entry and then backlash told me that the legs had entered the water by a different route from the hole which the arms and head made. A perfect entry, on the other hand, had a cleanness of sound about it which indicated complete control.

When something has given children pleasure, it is an extra joy to see it through their eyes, the scene brought to life by the fresh spontaneity of their excited comments. This is surely a fine way of getting vicarious visual pleasure. I still recall with relish my children's delight in the Christmas performances of *Toad of Toad Hall* at the

Stratford Memorial Theatre. The sound "poop-poop" produces an inevitable reply of "Fat face", with the recollection of conceited Mr. Toad and his discomfitures. Whenever I pass through a Swiss railway station, I remember the vivid description of these stations' colourful appearance contained in my children's exclamations and remarks as, too excited to sleep, they peeped through the window of our couchette compartment on our first family journey abroad.

An American publication I read some time ago took the view that a blind man should not expect services in the way of reading, and so on, from the members of his family. It seemed to imply that this was demeaning for them and him, that he should hire such services instead. On the contrary, I believe that these, like most forms of service, are ennobling and can legitimately be expected of members of a family, since they are or should be a team. The blind man, in return, should be ready to carry out any services that can be expected of him which contribute to the household's well-being. As soon as the children were old enough to do so, they would help me— generally with good grace!—by looking things up in dictionaries or encyclopaedias, for instance, and putting on tape vocabulary or sections of grammar of a new language I was learning. There is no doubt they benefited educationally!

Another American publication, *When You Meet a Blind Person* (a booklet published by the Allen County League for the Blind, Fort Wayne, Indiana), which I read during my recent trip to America, was a great deal more positive as a guide to the sighted for social and business contacts. Its introductory paragraph runs:

"Today or tomorrow you may meet someone who is blind. When you do, remember that he is an individual with his own distinct personality. He knows he cannot see and he has probably become used to the fact. He can hear, walk, make decisions like you do and he is pursuing most of the same daily activities he engaged in as a sighted man. It is no miracle that he can tell the time by his own watch, dial the telephone or light his own cigarette. He does not have a sixth sense, but he has had to learn to use other senses such as touch or hearing more fully."

Here are some of the booklet's general suggestions, often putting points I have already discussed, but in what seems to me a very concise and sensible way:

"When greeting a person, take his hand. To him this is the same as a friendly smile. Tell him who you are so that he does not have to wonder to whom he is speaking . . . When addressing him when others are present, use his name, touch his arm or provide some similar cue by which he can tell that your greeting is intended for him and not someone else.

"When entering a room where there is a blind person, say something, if only a word, and if necessary let him know who you are. Also, it may be a good idea to tell him when you leave the room or group . . .

"Do not be afraid to speak to blind people or worry about saying the wrong thing . . . remember that a blind person is interested in much the same things that you find interesting. It is not necessary to avoid the subject of blindness but you need not substitute it for the weather. Use the word 'see' as much and as often as you would with a sighted person. You will find that this is perfectly natural for the blind person.

"When giving directions to a blind person, be sure you say 'right' and 'left' according to the way he is facing . . . Trying to give directions from a distance such as across the street or from your car may only distract and confuse him.

"Don't fail to offer assistance to a blind pedestrian who is crossing the street or boarding a trolley. It may be that your assistance has some time been rejected or even resented by a blind person who fancied he did not need your help. If so, remember many others do need it.

"When a blind person is entering a car, bus, train, going upstairs or about to sit down, he needs only to have his hand placed on some identifying part of the object such as door, railing or back of the chair, as he can then orientate himself and from there on can handle the situation by himself . . . In a restaurant offer to read the menu, and when you do, also read the prices.

"If a blind person is using a guide dog, remember that the dog is a working dog and must not be diverted from carrying out her very important job . . . Petting the dog or offering her food may distract her attention.

"Always ask a blind person if he wishes help. Many blind people can do things very easily for themselves and do not like being helped without first being asked."

And finally, a point I have already stressed both directly and by implication: "If you have a blind person in your family, home or neighbourhood, don't deprive him of a sense of accomplishment and feeling of personal worth by refusing to let him do things by himself."

In our affluent, artificial and semi-automated society, there is a good deal of concern over the problems of leisure. Basically this is a question of interests, for anyone keenly interested in something has generally no need to wonder how to fill his leisure time. The recent survey of blind people in the United States showed they had much the same leisure interests as sighted people. It is harder for them, of course, to play the role of passive spectator, and I wonder whether they may not have an advantage in this.

I gather there are lots of blind people who enjoy the cinema or television, where the first appeal is purely visual. Personally I have not had much enjoyment from the cinema since I was blinded, averaging about one film a year. I find the changes of scene confusing, and feel uncomfortable if the person with me has to whisper explanations which must be distracting to those around. On my few visits I have preferred to go without explanations as far as possible, getting any satisfaction I could from the film's soundtrack.

Admittedly I can still remember with pleasure most of the few films I have been to. With some of them, occasional scenes flash upon the inward eye when I think of the film. If I think of *Doctor in the House*, the scene where every nurse wears a flower springs to mind. If I think of *The Sound of Music*, I picture the novitiate nun singing on the mountainside, with the valley and the nunnery stretched out below; or the von Trapp family singing *Edelweiss* at the festival. *Cheaper by the Dozen* brings back a memory of the hero and his family travelling in their little bus, or the scene at breakfast when the precocious youngster has answered a difficult question, causing father to say: "We'll *keep* that one."

Usually I prefer to go to the theatre, where there is less purely visual appeal and I can therefore enjoy the performance more on level terms with the sighted. I enjoy musicals too, especially if they have a good story, like *My Fair Lady* and *The Sound of Music*. *West Side Story* made a strong though rather painful impression on me, because I saw it soon after having two unpleasant experiences with gangs. A gang of six young "teds" had wandered into the youths' club on the evening of our weekly dance, apparently looking for trouble. They had been turned away at the door by Lena Eddy, our cashier, who wasn't prepared to stand any nonsense and had them sized up in a moment. But instead of going out they thought they would inspect another part of the building which led to the lounges and dining-rooms of the senior staff and directors. I was told about this, and went after them. My fury and the flashing metal cane I carried— which possibly they mistook for a sword stick—turned them into rabbits, and they fled down the eleven flights of stairs to the street below, with me in angry pursuit. It didn't occur to me until afterwards how awkward it might have been had they been really vicious characters. We got three of these a few weeks later. They attacked one of our members in the street outside the club, had him down on the ground and were punching him. Just then Ray Denton turned up, one of our older members and a very useful athlete. A few well-aimed blows quickly turned the young toughs into cowards, and they fled. Such episodes were rare, but the thought of what might have happened certainly increased the tension of *West Side Story* for me.

The wireless is absolutely suited to use by the blind, the appeal being entirely through the ear, so that you lose nothing unless a programme is accompanied by printed texts. I found this rather frustrating in the case of language programmes, and made representations to the B.B.C. to try to secure that such programmes would at least give the vocabulary aloud as well as in the printed text. The reply said there was not time to do this and one could obtain Braille copies made of the printed text; but I still feel that the programmes would gain if they included the spoken vocabulary of new words.

For a year or two after I had been blinded, I much preferred the spoken programmes of plays, talks and discussions. It was as though I felt the need for human contact which music did not seem to provide. Later, however, I found my appreciation of music much more developed than when I had my sight. Beethoven, in particular, assumed a new and deeper significance. The inner tranquillity of the quiet passages in the symphonies, and the triumphant passages of the final movements, had the same uplifting effect as one of Milton's nobler passages. They ran parallel to the unconquerable spirit exemplified in *Areopagitica*, "Let Truth and Falsehood grapple. Who ever knew Truth to be worsted in an encounter?" Beethoven seems to say, "I may be going deaf, or I may be deaf, but I can still hear beautiful music and give it to the world."

It may seem ludicrous, just after talking about Beethoven, to mention my own efforts in making music—on the piano, guitar, harmonica or piano accordion. But playing, with however little talent, has given me enjoyment and helped to lift my spirit, getting feelings of dissatisfaction and disquiet out of the system.

The blind have benefited greatly since the war from the development of the multi-tape talking book, a by-product of St. Dunstan's research towards a possible reading machine; though I personally have not been able to spare much time for such reading. The machine is about the size of a small record-player. It houses a metal cassette about twelve inches by six by two, which contains twenty or so tapes, representing the average length of a book. The controls are extremely simple: there is a switch-on, switch-off control on the outside of the instrument; the cassette fits on to a circular knob in the centre of the instrument; and a stop-go lever operates the tape after the cassette has been fitted. At the end of each track, the user is warned on the reading to stop the machine, press the button on the cassette which lines up the next tape, turn the cassette over, and re-start. The readings, by well-known actors and radio or television personalities, are excellent.

Although the instrument is apparently superior to anything else of its kind in the world, it has not been adopted by other countries, and it seems a pity there is not more co-operation in such matters so that the books could be readily interchangeable between countries, particularly, of course, Britain and the United States. I have blind friends in America who feel very strongly that vested interests are preventing them from having the use of this British machine.

My general reading has been limited during the last twenty-two years. I regret this, but the business of keeping up with essential reading has left little time for other kinds. The radio and theatre have helped, however, to prevent my getting completely out of touch with modern literature. Reading history has hardly been possible at all, but visits to places of historical interest have to some extent made up for it. I lose no opportunity of visiting factories and other focal points of present-day life so that I can be as thoroughly aware as possible of the real world I live in.

Other leisure pursuits which have helped towards a full life have been the reading of Braille magazines, walking, conversation and the company of friends, associated with a modest enjoyment of good food and wine. Of course the visual pleasures of the table are missing, although it may sometimes be an advantage not being able to see what you are going to eat. Once when I was encouraging some of our club members to be adventurous and tackle a dish which contained "calmares" (squid), one of them commented: "It's all right for you. You don't have to look at it."

For the blind even more than the sighted—because of the inevitable limitations on their movements—regular exercise every day is important in maintaining normal physical fitness. My efforts have not stopped me getting overweight, but I still feel the benefit of the "daily dozen".

The blind are often lonely. They have difficulty in establishing casual contacts. They may be restricted by lack of mobility, especially the old, who are in the majority of our blind population, sixty per cent being over sixty. Often the old cannot do very much about this lack, although there are a few splendid clubs giving a limited number of them tremendous help. But the rest of the blind population could have more done for them than some folk would admit, for example, by the extension of mobility training.

"No man is an island." Having benefited so greatly through others' work, I have tried to make some return by engaging in voluntary work of various kinds, mainly concerned with young people. This has brought its own rewards in friendships, the broadening of experience, and some unexpected memorable occasions; for instance, Margaret and I were twice privileged to visit Buckingham Palace.

The first time was at a presentation of Gold Badges to participants in the Duke of Edinburgh's Award Scheme; after the presentation Lord Hunt (then Sir John Hunt) took us to an ante-room to be presented to Prince Philip, and we chatted for a few minutes about his Scheme. The second time was at a party for the Commonwealth Conference of the Royal Life Saving Society. While I was being presented to the Queen and my wife to Prince Philip, it was obvious to Margaret that he was trying to remember where he had seen me before quite recently. Later in the evening he recalled the occasion at Bournville when I had been responsible for the arrangements on a short visit he had made.

As far as a full life goes, I must always come back to my own great good fortune in the enjoyment of a harmonious family life amidst a group of close and well-tried friends. Some friendships, like those with the Bannisters and the Pillings, go back to my schooldays, but most are part of the new life which started with our setting up house in Birmingham. High among these newer friends are Phyllis Muscott, who became Andrew's godmother, and Brandon and Flavia Cadbury, who paid me the great compliment of asking me to be godfather to Rebecca, their youngest child. The interest and support of all these and other friends have meant more to me than I can express here, sustaining me in meeting the manifold demands of "the trivial round, the common task".

# CHAPTER 11

## TRAVELLING BLIND

The degree of independent mobility attained by blind people varies tremendously. Some travel the world with the absolute minimum of assistance. Others hardly put one foot in front of another without help, even in the most sheltered environment. The reasons for wanting to be able to get about alone are as varied as the individuals themselves. In my own case, once Colonel Marks had suggested to me that it was a thing I ought to be doing, it appeared to be as normal as breathing. It became something I just had to do. The questions to be answered were: how could it be accomplished in safety, and without endangering other people? What were the limits of independent travel? They are questions which are being asked more than ever before.

Marjorie Dixon had presented me with my first stick, an ordinary walking stick which had belonged to her father. It had a sentimental attachment which made me keep it, even after it had been patched with a metal sleeve and was not really fit to be used. This "attachment" settled the question as to whether or not I should carry a white stick, although I suppose I could always have had it painted white. People did suggest that I ought to carry a white stick: to do so was only fair to other people; it gave them warning that they must take a little more care; it was a protection to me and to them, and more especially it was a signal all motorists recognised.

I accepted the argument, but said that I carried my badge of blindness in the sealed right eye socket and the closed left eye. The white stick was a negative status symbol, associated with a long-standing tradition of the poor blind man. I would do my utmost to ensure that I caused the least possible risk or inconvenience to those who failed to recognise at once that I was blind. I exonerated all motorists in advance, should any happen to hit me. If, in making my way about alone, I happened to bump into anyone, I would be quick and sincere with my apology, even when, as so very often happens, the person with sight was not making use of that advantage. But my ordinary and somewhat battered walking stick would be my silent protest against the poor-blind-man tradition, my mute invocation that I should be treated as an ordinary person, and not one to be pitied or regarded as inadequate. For other reasons, which I shall come to later, I am now prepared to carry a white stick, but the reaction of strangers requires more patient acceptance than I could have shown twenty years ago. There is still a great deal to be done to establish the right relationship between the sighted world and the blind.

Of course, the other possibility was to have a guide dog. I gave this idea very serious thought. I knew of the magnificent work being done at the Guide Dog Centre at Leamington Spa. The English love their dogs, and a guide dog would serve as a positive symbol, not a negative one; they were not associated with any negative tradition. Quite the contrary; their possession indicated a certain status, like possessing a motor car in the immediate post-war years. A dog, however, would be a considerable tie. She (most guide-dogs are female) would need constant care and attention and daily exercise, special arrangements at home, and when staying with friends, and in hotels. It might be difficult to keep her to myself with a small child in the house. What would happen to the dog if I went abroad?

Furthermore, the training period meant a whole month in residence at the Centre. The dog's working life was only eight years, and then the process would have to be repeated, and how would one feel about retraining when one was old? In normal circumstances there would be periodical heartbreaks, since a man's expectation of life is so much longer than a dog's. I didn't mind the risks and injuries of walking about alone so much as all that, provided I could get to where I wanted. The guide-dog argument was settled for me even before it was decided that I should go to work in a food factory, where a dog could not be used.

If I had been going to live in the country, or if I had not had a young family, my decision to choose a thirty-six inch walking stick instead of a dog might well have been different. A dog's companionship is often the answer to blind people who might otherwise be very lonely, and the dog helps greatly to solve the difficulties of navigation in open country.

Many people seem to have the idea that in some mysterious way a dog can divine where her master or mistress wants to go, and simply goes there. It is true that some dogs will take their owners over a few familiar routes to a destination indicated by a word, but the responsibility for navigation remains almost entirely with the handler. In towns, one of the biggest advantages of a dog is her ability to cope with traffic. In this country, however, the tremendous helpfulness of the public means that a blind person almost always finds someone around prepared to see him across a busy road. Observations of blind people in Nottingham showed that the average time a blind person waited for help in crossing was thirty seconds.

Learning how to cope with offers of help was, I found, one of the earliest lessons I had to learn in my endeavours to get about unaided. The helpful member of the public also has difficulty in knowing how or when to help.

> "O wad some Pow'r the giftie gie us
> To see oursels as others see us!"

The famous Burns couplet has often passed through my mind on this matter of the sighted offering help and the blind person accepting it. In conditions of present-day traffic, even self-dependent blind travellers are bound to need help sometimes. They should always remember that some of their less competent brethren are likely to need a great deal more help than they do. If they are ungracious in refusing offers of help, the person offering may be discouraged from making another offer to somebody in real need. The offer may be made clumsily at a moment when the blind traveller has been finding his journey a strain. Still, he has very probably had far more experience of dealing with sighted people than the other way round. The onus is therefore on him to show this superior experience by dealing appropriately with the sighted would-be helper. (As the booklet *When You Meet a Blind Person* shows, however, it can work the other way round too.)[1]

This applies in several ways. The would-be helper may be feeling a bit awkward and self-conscious. A few words of general conversation may help to disperse this feeling: some trivial comment, such as, "There seems to be rather more traffic about than usual." I mention traffic because the commonest situation when the blind person really needs help is in getting safely across a busy road. In such circumstances, he should also make sure the helper is on his side nearest to the oncoming traffic, so that there is no obstruction of vision. He should also see that the help is given in the most appropriate form. Generally, this will be ensured by his taking the escort's arm—in the case of a stranger, it is best for him to grip the arm just above the elbow. He can quickly break this grip if he wants to. Going up or down stairs, or in complex situations where manoeuvre is necessary, it is best to grip the escort's wrist.

If nobody offers help, the blind person may need to attract it. If there are several people about, he should make sure the help is given specifically. He might do this by grazing someone walking past, making his apology, and following this with the request for help.

If there are not many people about, he may need to attract attention by tapping his stick or holding up his stick. Often blind people stand by the edge of a footpath, and just wait. On occasions when I have been waiting for a friend, or simply standing away from the road, listening, and building up by the sound my picture of what is around, I have had many people come up to me and offer help. Some of them have seemed most disappointed when I declined their offer with thanks and explained what I was doing.

Perhaps there should be a generally accepted convention which says, in effect: "I am a blind person needing assistance." In the case of blind people carrying sticks or canes, they might adopt a pose, holding the stick by the shaft, raised a foot or two from the ground so that the crook is about shoulder level, with the forearm parallel to the ground. This position does not seem to me too unnatural

[1] See para. 5, page 134.

or conspicuous; but it could be easily recognised, and is a position a blind person would not normally assume. Adopting this convention would help sighted and blind alike. The former would not be in any doubt that they should respond to their impulse to help.

Embarrassment is often caused when a well-meaning but masterful sighted person seizes someone who is blind, and starts to propel him, even before the blind person has confirmed that he wants help. This is the moment when the blind traveller must call on all his experience, self-restraint and patience. He may even find it necessary to drop his arm to break the grip which has been taken of it; if, for example, it is his stick arm which has been seized and he needs to use it to stop himself stumbling against an anticipated obstacle. Some people assume that, because they can see a situation, they know what is in the blind person's mind and what he must do. They may be completely wrong, and it is always preferable if the sighted person asks whether he can help.

A common fault which sighted people make in giving help is that they tend to be too vigorous about it. There is the bus conductor who tries to help his descending passenger by gripping him strongly as he steps off the bus. This is likely to throw the passenger off balance. If any grip is needed, it can be quite light—and this can always be increased if necessary.

When I was quite a small boy, we were taught in school that we should help the old and disabled. It would perhaps have been as well if we had also been given a little instruction on how to help. I remember asking a blind man if I should see him across the road. I still remember the look of displeasure which crossed his face when I gripped his arm, probably because I was gripping it a good deal more tightly than was necessary. The blind person may or may not need to be steered, but this should be done with a fairly loose grip; in any case, as I have said, the better arrangement is for the blind person to grip his escort's arm.

This is particularly the case if the escorting is going to last for some time or is over uneven terrain or places where there are steps up and down. It rather depends on the relative heights of the two people involved, but usually much the best method, in the case of friends or relatives, is for the blind person to pass his arm through his companion's arm, so that the hand rests on the forearm. This puts the blind person slightly behind the escort, so that a little advance notice is given of variations from the straight or level. The escort should pause at the top of a flight of steps, and mention that there are steps down.

It is remarkable that some people do not realise how important it is for the person being escorted to know whether steps are up or down. Often escorts try to estimate the number of steps, generally inaccurately. When being escorted on steps down, I prefer to keep my stick down and slightly in front of me, so that I have warning of the last step. Going up steps, I have found it helpful to use my stick to touch the edge of the step two ahead of me, which helps me to gauge the height of the steps, and also gives warning of the approach of the top.

I recall a friend who carried a short leather strap. When he was escorting a blind young lady for some distance, each held one end of the strap, making guidance possible without any contact, a method which might recommend itself in hot weather. An Austrian professor showed me the method adopted in that country, which is to link little fingers. I did not feel that this method gave the same quickness or accuracy of information as the method of gripping the forearm.

I also remember a St. Dunstaner colleague who stated that in Europe people regard you as sighted unless you carry a white stick. They would still do so, he said, "even if you were carrying your head under your arm." This has not been my experience. It would be interesting to compare the attitudes towards blind people in different countries; so far as I am aware, no study of this kind has been made. Certainly, I doubt if the helpfulness of the British public towards the blind is likely to be exceeded anywhere in the world.

I have heard it suggested that the attitude in the U.S.A. is often one of indifference. In a brief visit of six weeks I did not find this, although Don Blasch of Western Michigan University told me a story of a blind student who had to abandon a university course—he did not say which university it was—because he could not get himself to and from his classes. Don used this as an argument for mobility training, but I felt the story reflected badly on the other students of that university.

Special situations which can make things difficult for escorts are getting into vehicles and moving among obstacles in a congested environment. Getting into a car, I find the easiest method is if my escort puts my hand on the handle of the door. It is then easy to discover which way the car is pointing, to open the door, feel the top of the aperture and then the seat, and so avoid any risk of bumping my head or awkwardness in getting in. During the first year of my blindness, I had not acquired this technique, and made an awful fool of myself when I fell into a Daimler outside a famous London hotel, finishing up in a heap on the floor of the limousine. It is often helpful if the escort tells you which way the car is pointing, but as you acquire experience in these matters with a familiar escort, this ceases to be necessary. My wife knows that she only needs to tell me where the car is. If I approach it from the front, I feel the windscreen and use that as my position indicator to find the handle. Getting out, you need to make sure there are no passing pedestrians who might be struck by the opening door nor, indeed, any obstacle such as a lamp-post or parking meter.

Moving in a congested area with obstacles, it is better to grip the escort's wrist or hand, and follow behind. In doing this, you have to be rather careful not to get too near, with the danger of stepping on the escort's foot.

Going through revolving doors, it is preferable to follow your escort in the next "compartment", and I find it helpful to run the back of my curled fingers along the frame against which the edge of the door runs.

When using escalators, it is helpful if the escort pauses at the top, and puts one hand on the moving rail. Going down, I hold my stick and press slightly against the step I am standing on. As the escalator levels out I press down a little more firmly to step off. Going up, I hold my stick against the wall of the step immediately above the one I am being carried on. Again, the levelling-out gives me the signal to step off.

Some buses have an upright rail near the edge of the boarding deck. I find the easiest way of boarding such a bus is if my wife puts my hand against this rail; my stick tells me how high the step is. If we are descending from the top of a bus, my wife goes first, stops at the top of the stairs, and puts my hand on the rail. I always like to use rails or bannisters when they are available. They give you a good deal of information about where you are. If it is a building, for example, it is quite remarkable how much the rail can tell you. The carved stone rail of a medieval house staircase in Lyon is as eloquent as the modern finish of the thermoplastic-covered metal handrails in the Palais des Congrés in that city.

There are many blind people who regard a stick as unnecessary when being escorted. Personally, I find it a useful extra precaution, particularly if I am being steered in a dangerous area by an in-experienced person. There was one classic occasion at Portsmouth, when I was going over an aircraft carrier with a group of our club members, one of whom was acting as my guide. We were walking along part of the vessel when I felt space on my right where there should have been deck. I asked my guide about it. "Oh," he said, "that's the part where they store the 'planes." Since we were walking along the side of a deep steep drop, I was glad that I had not veered as we walked.

With an experienced escort, I find that using my stick can ease the burden of escorting. You have to be continually on your guard, however, that the stick does not get in other people's way. I also use it as an "environmental perceptor" to tell me a little more about the area we are passing through, although this too is something which has to be done with discretion.

The traditional idea of a blind person finding his way about alone is that of somebody walking along tapping the wall, or some similar guide line, with his white stick. Like all my blinded fellows, when I first tried to move about outside on my own, I started by making quite a noise as I banged my way about, no doubt seeking reassurance from the noise I was making. This phase gives way to one where the blind person seeks a much more unobtrusive technique. A good many blind people will not use a stick of any sort, because they feel it brands them and makes them conspicuous. It is true that in some cases people do not recognise them as blind, but the self-dependent mobility they achieve is slow and limited. They tend to be confined to routes they have learnt and to fairly protected conditions. While the unobservant sighted person may not recognise them as blind, they are nevertheless noted as different and somewhat odd.

In some educational circles concerned with blind children the use of a stick is deprecated. The argument is that the children will come to be dependent on a stick. I find this argument about as sensible as suggesting that someone with defective vision should not wear spectacles. A stick is a three-foot extension of the arm and of the tactile sense. It is a simple means of securing more information about one's environment.

The tactile sense is the one the blind person invariably uses when uncertain of the interpretation produced from using his other senses. I suppose it is for this reason that I dislike holding things when I have finished using them, such as an empty cup and saucer. Without having given conscious thought to it, I have had this disinclination ever since I was blinded. It has probably derived from the feeling that my sensory capacity was being limited unnecessarily. A stick is sometimes the only safe way of making sure the ground is where you want to place your feet in order to avoid discomfort or danger. I have also come to the conclusion that it is wasted effort for any totally blind person to try to give the continuous impression of having sight. He is much more likely to win the respect of his sighted fellows if he concentrates his energies on becoming a competent blind person than if he uses them trying to make people believe he can see.

I have already mentioned how, during my first year of blindness, I experimented with various methods of using the stick; and how in the end, partly because I wanted to appear as normal as possible, and partly because it fitted in with walking at something like my old speed of three miles an hour, I generally used the ordinary method of swinging a walking stick, extending the swing a little to the side if I wished to maintain contact with a guiding wall or hedge. In more congested areas, where there were more likely to be obstacles, I held the stick in front of me, just clear of the ground, rather like an elephant's trunk. It occurred to me several times that it might be useful to have a longer stick which I could run on the ground; and I even tried a little experiment with Andrew's Scout stick; but I thought such a method would be clumsy and conspicuous, and gave up the idea, although I did have a wheel fitted to one stick so that I could run it ahead of me. This too proved a failure.

If I thought I was approaching the top of a flight of stairs, or some other peril, I would run the stick on the ground, reaching forward. Generally the method proved more or less safe, but it had the disadvantage of making me lean forward, and occasionally my head would find an unexpected obstacle. The usual injuries I suffered were bumps on the head, or at any rate these were the ones which hurt. Once I had learned to protect myself against cracks on the shin, other injuries did not seem worth bothering about—the occasional scraped hand or bang on the body. There were also the "kerb" injuries, stubbed toe on an up kerb, ankle cracked or spine jarred by a surprise down kerb.

I never restricted myself to routes I had learnt with the aid of a sighted friend or relation, so that I was always liable to the hazards mentioned; but we are all creatures of habit, and some of my routes became very familiar and the risk of injury very slight. The method was certainly fallible, however, especially in unknown areas, and whenever there was an unexpected and irrational variation in conditions. There is a lane a few hundred yards from my home, which is called Hole Lane. Twice the telephone engineers dug a six-foot-deep hole there, and left it unfenced. Twice I found myself unexpectedly standing in the hole, unhurt physically but feeling something a little stronger than "a gentle shock of mild surprise".

I confess that for some time afterwards I walked a bit tentatively when in the pitfall area, and although I felt a little foolish and self-conscious, ran my stick on the pavement to satisfy myself that the call of tea had not left another untended and unfenced hole. English law now requires protection to be given against dangers of this kind but I can never quite shed the thought that one careless workman might create a difficult situation. Generally there are several clues to give you warning that the terrain might have been altered—like the noise of work going on, loose soil on the footpath, or an alteration in the level of the pavement.

For a totally blind person to achieve independent mobility, certain qualities and faculties are indispensable. One is the determination to get about alone. Others are balance, sense of position in space, a good memory, kinaesthetic sense, ability to interpret the clues provided by hearing, touch and smell; and a capacity for gauging time and distance. He must at all times use all his faculties to remain familiar with his environment and interpret correctly the information which comes through to him. In recent years there has been a good deal of research into "obstacle sense" or "facial vision". These terms describe a person's ability to detect the presence of an object near him without touching it, and even though it is not emitting any smell, heat or audible sound. The research has shown that human beings can achieve a "ranging" of obstacles by using the sounds reflected or scattered from objects. Blind children apparently develop obstacle sense by the age of two; and it is a faculty the sighted can acquire. It doesn't work where there is a complete absence of sound or movement, and has only a limited value in helping blind people to get about. I find it much easier to detect some "objects" than others: lamp-posts, trees or cars are quite easy, for instance, but I may fail to detect a person standing still and silent directly in my path.

The first time I achieved "obstacle sense" was when I "spotted" the pillar-box in Watling Street, Church Stretton; and I have tried to develop the faculty ever since as much as possible. I have tended to concentrate on using the right ear, which has made it stand away from the side of my head more than the left ear—I am convinced of this, and Margaret has confirmed it by careful scrutiny of photographs taken of me before the war.

In detecting an obstacle blind people usually say they "feel" something there. When I have detected something, although it is really by reflected sound, I get the idea that there is a dark blur in the greyness before my eyes. After some painful experiences over the years, I am no doubt subconsciously afraid I may bump into something, and this leads, I believe, to the odd transference of sensations —since the obstacle does not physically cause the blur.

Obstacle sense is often accentuated, I have found, when the air is still, heavy and oppressive. It gives me a "feel" of having objects all round me, a disturbing sensation when I am not feeling on my best form.

In finding their way alone in town probably the most common aid to navigation blind people use is that of counting blocks or crossings, and remembering turns. This is supplemented by awareness of sound clues, such as the noise of traffic along a busy road, the sound or smell of a factory, music from a café, shop or dance-hall, the noises from a school, the chiming of clocks, the noise of rail traffic. There are distinctive "sound-marks", just as there are distinctive landmarks. The noise of a shop-door closing can be as distinctive as that of a *carillon*.

By carefully examining a small part of a district, a blind person can get as unique a concept of it as a sighted person by close visual scrutiny. Small areas will serve as unmistakable landmarks for the blind person who wishes to feel that he can travel on his own anywhere he likes in a particular district. Besides providing him with a valuable aid to navigation, this is a safeguard against getting lost, possibly within a short distance of his home. There is a real difficulty about carrying out such an examination if you are alone, because the first presumption of the sighted observer who notices you doing it is that you are lost and need assistance. When I am exploring completely new territory, and am asked whether I am lost, I use it as an opportunity for securing information like the name of a street, which might otherwise be inaccessible. It would be helpful if more authorities used waist-high street name-plates with raised letters as is done, I am glad to say, in my district.

Friends have often asked me: "How do you know when you have reached a corner and are about to cross a street, particularly if the pavement and the road merge?" This is an important question, especially for those blind travellers who do not keep their direction by following a wall, hedge or similar guide line. There are various answers depending on the circumstances. In the case of the pavement which merges with the road, you have to be on your guard to notice the difference in slope as the pavement meets the road and also to detect the camber as you approach the crown of the road. This supplements all the other information you can gather.

There may, for instance, be an obvious difference in reflected sound from buildings at the corner of a street. Pavements almost invariably have their own camber at the junction of two streets as the pavement slopes towards the road. The perceptive blind traveller, using his feet to give him this information, can follow a corner round by the use of this clue alone. He will probably have heard traffic as he approaches the street he wishes to cross. This will give him advance notice that he is approaching the end of the block. There may be other clues too, such as increased movement of air, sounds from right or left at the corner, walking out of shade into sun, or feeling the gap between the edging stone of the pavement and the one next to it.

In this country, where the sun is often not shining, or not strongly enough to penetrate the industrial haze, the blind walker can make only limited use of the sun as an aid to navigation. If he can feel its warmth, this will help him a good deal to avoid going round a corner, possibly a gradual one, without realising it. When he is exploring a new area, or re-establishing his position if temporarily lost, the position of the sun can also be a very helpful guide. So far no one has devised a satisfactory compass for a blind person to use when walking alone, although progress has been made with the radio compass.

Although, as mentioned several times, most people tap their way along a wall or other guide-line, this method is open to many objections. The resultant posture tends to be poor. There is always the danger of meeting obstacles and of straying off the line at openings like drives and garage entrances. In suburban areas there is the constant menace of overhanging hedges or bushes: it is most irritating to be slapped in the face by wet branches or soaked by brushing against a wet hedge. For these reasons I have always preferred, where possible, a method which enabled me to walk along the middle of a pavement.

A blind walker is bound to rely a great deal on his memory. This can be aided by the process of conscious visualisation, and he may also be spared some concentrated effort through the working of the kinaesthetic sense. By constant practice his muscles may be so well used to the effort needed in assessing the short distance from the corner of a block to an office entrance, say, that he can do it without having to count paces or follow a guide line.

Over very short distances counting paces may be the only easy alternative to laboriously following a guide line. Over longish distances along a straight road, I have sometimes found it useful to time myself, especially on a new route where I didn't want to be bothered with checking the things which might have indicated my position.

Until recent years a good deal of strain was inevitable for a blind person walking alone. I shall come later to the methods which have been devised for relieving this strain. Even with aids, the blind traveller cannot afford to daydream or let his thoughts wander too far from the business of getting about safely and efficiently.

This was brought home to me quite lately. I was walking along the top floor of the dining block at Bournville, having gone up there by the lift. Suddenly I found myself in mid-air. In a moment of absent-mindedness, I had turned right from the lift instead of walking straight forward. I must have been walking rather quickly, because I reached the landing at the foot of the six steps in one step; I was unhurt. I remember telling myself to stay upright as I flew through the air—a drill I have found useful once or twice before when unexpectedly coming across steps down. On these occasions, however, I was not going so quickly, and was able to walk down the stairs, if in rather a hurry.

The few times I have fallen down stairs have been when I was being escorted, and they have made me thankful that I learned to fall as a youngster when I was learning to skate. It was probably also while learning to skate that I discovered that the chances of remaining upright on slippery ground are increased if you walk keeping the feet as close to the ground as possible between steps.

The feet, being in constant touch with the environment, are rich sources of information. Besides detecting slope, curve and gaps, they tell you a great deal about the nature of the surface you are walking on, so long as the mind is active in interpretation. For example, feeling grit walked or kicked on to a pavement from a footpath may be the easiest way of telling when you should turn to find that footpath. Sometimes the nature of the road or path surface can provide an unmistakable clue to your whereabouts. In Birmingham, for example, a rubber road surface shows that you are near Lewis's stores. Incidentally, thinking of the use of the feet, if I drop anything on a dirty surface such as a pavement and have to look for it, I much prefer to look with my feet than with my hands.

Special difficulties of orientation or navigation arise under certain conditions. Loud noise, besides being a possible source of fear in itself, is disquieting because it tends to mask the warning noises of the immediate vicinity; although it can be useful as a guide, either in itself or in its reflections from a guiding wall surface. This has been demonstrated by the research of Dr. J. P. Wilson of Keele University in his examination of "human ranging" using ambient or self-generated sound.

Traffic sounds can be a most valuable aid to orientation, but the ever expanding volume of fast-moving traffic is certainly an increasing deterrent to the blind pedestrian, as mentioned earlier. There is no problem in this country if he wishes to cross a road and there are people around: help is sure to be readily available if he indicates his need of it. If there are no people about, he must practise a very careful safety drill as a matter of unfailing routine when crossing roads. Features of this routine are: careful-listening to determine the position, direction, and speed of moving vehicles; checking to ensure that he is about to make the shortest possible crossing; indicating clearly by raising the stick arm his intention to cross; crossing without hesitation and at a measured and deliberate pace once he has decided to move.

I have come across motorists who stopped, kept their engine running, and called to me to cross. They did not appreciate that this made me feel insecure because the noise of their engine had a masking effect. In such circumstances I do not move until I have established that there is no chance of an overtaking car failing to realise why the motorist has stopped, or of my failing to detect a car moving fast in the opposite direction owing to the noise of the helpful motorist's engine.

High wind and driving rain are conditions the blind traveller finds difficult; they may make him feel he needs the help of contact with some sort of guide line. There is no doubt, however, that conditions of thick snow are the most difficult. This is the blind man's fog. It can give a baffling uniformity to the landscape, or windblown snow may transform the contours. Roads and pavements in towns can be merged and hidden under the snow. Echoes and ambient sounds are muffled or deadened, making obstacle detection more difficult. In the country it is impossible to find paths, and roads can be indistinguishable from the surrounding fields.

Friends living in cities in the United States assure me that they have no difficulty in making their way about alone, because pavements and roads are cleared. In this country, where such snow clearing is much less an automatic routine, I have always found it pretty difficult unless I got my stick through the snow to find something which could act as a point of orientation: for example a pavement as distinct from a grass verge.

To avoid the unpleasantness of getting my shoes filled with snow I wear waterproof climbing boots, which also keep the feet warm and so better able to interpret information which comes through to them. Ridged rubber soles also help to ensure that I keep my foothold.

If it is difficult to detect the pavement, I may walk in the road and follow a kerb, or I may walk on the pavement and try to follow a guiding line. If I do the latter I am liable to walk into obstacles which are harder to detect because of the conditions, or to be wiped across the face by snow-laden shrubs or trees—which add to one's discomfort by cascading snow down one's neck. If the roads have been cleared, it may be possible to walk in the road, using the camber as guide or perhaps the heaped-up snow, and getting into the side if any traffic approaches. Under such conditions, however, walking in the road may be an unwarranted risk because of the danger of cars skidding.

Until the advent of the sonar torch, which I will deal with later, I walked alone under such conditions as little as I possibly could. It was always a real strain, and there was the danger of getting lost even within a short distance of my home. This once happened, and my peace of mind was not improved by the knowledge that there is a deep and unfenced pool some two hundred yards away from my house. On another occasion we had had a heavy fall of snow with deep drifting. I set out to walk to the bus, but gave up the attempt when I found myself in a neighbour's garden, apparently seeking entry through his lounge window.

With regard to travel in its wider sense, I have heard people say that its attractions must be much smaller for the blind than for the sighted. This assumes that a large part of the enjoyment in travel comes from satisfying the visual sense—a view I could never accept. No doubt there are scenes on which it is a soul-purifying experience to gaze. A blind traveller will be fortunate indeed if he can catch from a gifted, sighted escort the awe-inspiring grandeur of the Himalayas, the fiery beauty of the sun setting in the Western Isles, or the tranquil loveliness of the Taj Mahal. He cannot appreciate to the full the architectural splendours of Florence, the wonder of the Parthenon, or the futuristic achievement of Brazilia. There are lots of people with normal vision, however, on whom such sights are wasted; and the blind man may well have developed an extra sensitivity, thus feeling and perceiving some things which the sighted miss.

As a boy I saw Notre Dame in Paris, the sombre mass of its towers rising from the Ile de la Cité and dominating the Seine. My boyhood memory of it has faded, but when I am there, I feel the atmosphere just as strongly. Having walked at night through the magic of a pine forest in the Harz mountains, I can understand how some Germans become almost superstitiously romantic. Standing on the top of the Arc de Triomphe, you do not have to see Paris's traffic to appreciate its Gallic abandon. Walking in Las Ramblas or the Plaza Cataluna in Barcelona, you can absorb the animation of the scene late on a summer's night without needing to see the gayness of the flower stalls or the coloured fountains.

Sight may possibly enhance the pleasures of fast movement, but I find I still enjoy moving fast as much as before I was blinded—except in one context. In the last twenty-two years I have only once been on a fairground switchback, and that was its British archetype, the Big Dipper at Blackpool. I went with Andrew, then about seven, and counted myself lucky to survive. I think it was the impossibility of gauging when the switches from ascent to descent were going to take place; but I was convinced I should be thrown out before the thing finished its succession of shocks and strains. Nothing untoward happened, and Andrew was quite unaware of my silent terror, but I declined his suggestion that we should stay on for a second round—and made up my mind never to repeat the experience.

Riding in a car with an obviously incompetent driver, who is always stopping suddenly and without warning, can also be an ordeal, and I am very glad safety belts are being made compulsory on new cars: they are very relaxing and reassuring to the blind passenger. Even when riding in a closed car, by the way, a blind person can use his senses to the full, gauging its speed by the various sounds, tyres on the road, engine noise, flow of air past the windscreen, and perhaps vibration noises too. He can easily get a "feedback" by checking the speed with the driver.

For me, some types of motion bring even greater delight in retrospect. Among many examples, I still recall the incomparable smoothness of a journey by pleasure-boat across Lake Lucerne, after climbing to the top of Pilatus by a bumpy, enclosed funicular railway, and coming down by cable car. There is the remembered smoothness of the first welded railway lines I travelled on—just north of Barcelona. There is the thrill of the seat pushing into your back as the Boeing 707 takes off, almost standing on its tail; the echoing clatter which tells you that the Orient Express is passing through the Simplon Tunnel on its way from Milan to Paris; the flying spray and the surging water below your feet when waterskiing in the warm Mediterranean; the pressure against the feet and the crown of the head as the lift speeds to the top of the Empire State

Building in New York; the song of the wind through the strut of the glider above the Longmynd in Shropshire; and so I could go on.

Because I could only partially enjoy the spectacles which different countries had to offer, I was all the more anxious to learn something of their languages so as to increase the possibilities of contact with their people. The satisfaction of successful communication adds to the pleasures of a country's specialities of cuisine and cellar.

There seems no evidence to suggest that blindness makes the palate more sensitive in the way that trying to achieve an effective obstacle sense leads to a more subtle perception through hearing. But the pleasures of the table can certainly be a permanent and unfailing satisfaction for blind people who take good care of their health and digestion.

When someone takes me out for a drive, I appreciate his describing things for me as we go, but one can only absorb so much from words and he may well not realise how much it means to me if we stop now and then to walk round for a little. Although the amount of information coming through my own senses may be small, it does give me the "feel" of the surroundings, and helps enormously to make the experience real, vivid and lasting for me.

Travel by bus is an art in itself. The first requirement is to be able to find the bus-stop easily and naturally. If sighted help is available, I use it to learn the topography of the area round the bus-stop, allowing for "overshooting" and "undershooting"; also the areas round the next stops before and after the one I wish to use. If possible I supplement this knowledge by investigating the district on my own, preferably at a quiet time when there are few people around.

"First catch your fish" is a good motto. The bus-stop you use may be served by several buses operating on different routes. You may be able to distinguish the bus you want by the sound of its engine, but probably it will not be distinctive enough for that. If there are people about, you can ask them which bus is approaching, so that you don't make a bus pull up unnecessarily. If there aren't any people, the only thing to do is stop the bus and check before getting on that it is the right one.

It is a good thing to learn the different types of buses on the service you use, and to note any characteristic features on boarding which confirm that you have got on the right bus: for example the number of steps into it, the presence or absence of doors, the method of closing them, the presence or absence of a pay point just inside, and a variety of other items. If you recognise the type of bus, it will remind you of the seating lay-out, so that you can look for a seat without fumbling. Generally someone helps me to a vacant seat, or tells me where there is one; but if not, I follow the seats on my right until I find a vacant one. I have never had to come back along the other side to find an empty seat, because I am always told the position before I get to the end of the right-hand side.

If the bus is crowded and someone offers me a seat, I accept immediately and with thanks. I may well be as capable of standing as the person who has offered the seat, but I am much more likely to get in the way of others.

On a route you use regularly, you can normally devise a system for knowing where the bus is at any given moment. As a rule there are plenty of clues. The most obvious will be right-angled turns; but you can also distinguish marked ascents or descents, roads which cross and carry constant traffic, the different sounds made by different road surfaces, distinctive noises en route such as striking clocks, the noises made by the bus as it passes through changing areas of open or enclosed space, points where normally lots of people get on or off, bumps in the road as the bus crosses an intersecting road with a pronounced camber, points where the camber is steep or the bus is struck by overhanging branches, or changes in the sound of the tyres on different road surfaces.

Getting off a bus presents special problems for the blind traveller. As the route becomes more familiar, and he tends to think of other things instead of following it, he needs to have a method of avoiding missing his stop. When I am travelling to work, my safety warning signal is a turn to the left. If this is not followed by a turn to the right within twelve seconds, I know that it is time to get off. On the return journey, the warning signal is a weave to the left, followed by a weave to the right, as the bus negotiates a roundabout.

When preparing to get off, it is essential to know the interior of the bus, so that you know where the points are to grip and protect yourself against the sudden lurch or stop. Getting off, you have to be careful not to bump into people, or into the unexpected hazard of a lamp-post or bus-stop.

These points of technique become a daily pattern which needs no thought or effort if you set out to make them a matter of habit.

When travelling alone on trains, I have usually had luggage with me, and so have used a porter. It saves trouble if I find out in which direction the train will be travelling; on my own I still can't be sure of that direction unless I take very careful note when the train moves forward—or backward, of course, depending on which seat I am occupying, and whether the train shunts backward on to a fresh line before moving off on its journey.

I also ask the porter where the toilets and the dining car are, and how many coaches away the latter is. If the dining car is several coaches away, I slip a rubber band over the compartment door handle, and count the number of coaches as I make my way to the diner. Probably I know the number of the compartment and the coach, so that it is very unlikely I shall be unable to find my compartment again after visiting the dining car. Similarly, when going to the toilet, I sometimes make things easier by the rubber-band technique, besides counting the paces from my compartment; and I also use the rubber-band in hotels where I might want an easy check that I have come to the right door.

Generally on a train there are fellow travellers who are only too ready to offer help and information. Sometimes, however, particularly at night, you may be alone in a compartment, and it is a good thing to have a system to make sure you complete the journey without risk or embarrassing error. A knowledge of the timetable schedule, the use of the Braille watch and interpretation of the sound clues usually provide the answers. If, for example, you are travelling to a large town, and a few minutes before the scheduled time of arrival the train bumps over a sequence of points, it is a fair supposition that you are approaching your destination. Doors need to be opened with special caution, and I always make a point of listening very carefully to the noises from the platform before opening a railway carriage door. This helps to avoid anyone being caught by it and to tell you whether the train has reached the platform. Before trying to get out, I make sure the platform is indeed there, feeling for it with my stick. I remember once coming into Birmingham on a practically empty train, when I was surprised to find the train had not quite stopped, but was gliding silently forward. I might have been in trouble if I had already started getting out! The only time I have had to ask for help to find my compartment again after visiting the dining car was on a holiday visit to Spain with a group of our young factory workers, who were still sleeping on my return from early breakfast. When I take such groups abroad, I make a Braille copy of the itinerary and timetable, and carry the journey and reservation tickets in envelopes on which I have Brailled the appropriate information. The first of such journeys which I made in 1949 provided an incident I shall always remember.

We were en route for the work-camp at Fontenay-aux-Roses, just outside Paris, which I mentioned earlier. Dieppe still showed many signs of war damage. There was no station platform, and I stood on the ground outside the door of our reserved coach, checking the party in. One of the group had taken my bag, and said he would come back for me when he had deposited it. The scene outside the other side of the coach was so interesting that he forgot I was waiting for him. I did not heed the warning from one of the French passengers to get aboard, and suddenly I heard the train moving. I thought to myself: "Well, this is a fine thing. Supposed to be in charge of a party, and I get left on the platform at Dieppe, holding the party ticket." The coach slowly moved past me. A Spanish refugee, Elvio Garcia, quick-witted and an excellent games player, was standing in the open doorway. "Dive for it!" he shouted. I felt for the doorway, and dived. He hauled me aboard where I received the abject apologies of my forgetful young friend.

Spanish trains in the early post-war years were liable to have no doors. I made this discovery on a train going from Sitges to Barcelona, and was glad my technique for getting around in unfamiliar circumstances was proof against such surprises.

The same might apply to other experiences in Europe, several connected with Spain, where solidity is not the prime characteristic of the installations. Within a few hours of booking-in at the first hotel I had stayed at in that country, I went to the toilet and walked into a washbasin just inside the door, in a position where it was almost impossible to avoid it. I was surprised at the encounter, but astonished at the sequel. The thing detached itself from the wall, and crashed to the tiled floor in smithereens.

On the subject of toilets and bathrooms, it is remarkable what a variety of arrangements there can be—setting the blind traveller an equal variety of problems. It is sometimes a matter of safety, but more often of developing a system for finding things without embarrassment.

Glass shelves and glass tumblers may be sited in the most unlikely places, and great ingenuity has been shown in devising ways of operating the lavatory flush. Nobody as yet seems to have thought of introducing press-button, electrically controlled systems; but what with rotating knobs in the side of the wall, foot pedals, levers, chains, small handles, large handles, low position, high position, obvious location, concealed location—a blind person may well have to go through a very systematic search operation.

Being unable to see the behaviour of those round them, the blind may often have difficulty with points of etiquette. In such matters, particularly when in a different country, the wise course is to seek advice from those qualified to give it. The same applies to appearance. It is always specially important for the blind to be careful about this. In their own country it matters because of the image they present to their sighted fellows. Abroad it becomes doubly important.

From questions of social orientation my thoughts turn to the business of physical orientation. Simple maps which I could read have proved useful over the years in helping me to get an idea of the plan of a city, a village, or even a complicated street lay-out. Using the Sewell Raised Line Drawing Kit, which produces narrow raised lines on thin sheets of plastic paper, Margaret has made simplified plans of places such as Paris, Barcelona, and Sitges, which have helped considerably to build up my picture. They have been rather hard to read, however—much harder than the embossed dot outlines on Braille paper which Margaret has made of sections of a local street plan: these have given me an accurate idea of difficult areas. The plastic maps produced by The Royal National Institute for the Blind are one example of the increasing attention paid in recent years to this facet of helping people to "travel blind".

CHAPTER 12

## SENSORY AIDS

Early in June 1962 I happened to be seated next to Lady Fraser at the Reunion lunch of St. Dunstaners resident in the Birmingham area. Towards the end of the meal I asked: "Have any new developments taken place lately?"

"There is one thing," said Lady Fraser. "It's frightfully hush-hush. It's an ultra-sonic gadget for detecting obstacles. It's the invention of a chappie in the Electrical Engineering Department at Birmingham University." "Really?" I said. "I'd rather like to try it. Do you remember when Ted and I tried out the device at Church Stretton which Professor Beurle had invented? I shall never forget how we swiped the reader, Tony, thinking we had discovered an obstacle."

After lunch I had a word with Sir Ian Fraser, who agreed to arrange that I should be given an opportunity of trying the acoustic aid, as it was then called. He told me that the inventor was a Dr. Leslie Kay; so, a day or two later, when I was with my friend Ken Bannister, now a Professor at Birmingham University, I mentioned that I would like to meet Dr. Kay. Ken got in touch with him and it was arranged that we should have lunch together. Dr. Kay brought along an aid, and gave me a brief demonstration. He told me he had been supported in producing this prototype by a firm called "Ultra Electronics" in conjunction with St. Dunstan's and the National Research Development Council.

I have never been anything of a technician, and my scientific knowledge is extremely limited. I could, however, understand enough of what it was about to grasp the basic principle. Essentially, the apparatus was a transistorised transmitter-receiver. It put out an ultra-sonic beam, which was reflected back by objects in its path. The difference in time between the transmitted and received signals produced a difference in frequency, which resulted in a signal heard in two plastic earpieces. Leslie Kay held one of the earpieces, and I the other. The bleep-like signals came through bafflingly often. It was like listening to a new language conjured from the atmosphere. It was new and exciting, but I felt utterly bewildered.

I was due to go off to Spain in a few days' time with a group of our factory club members, and suggested that it would be useful if I could take an aid out with me, as I should probably have time to try it out in the evenings. Unfortunately there was not a spare model available, but soon after my return I received a letter from Sir Ian Fraser informing me that he had arranged for me to have one for trial.

It was given to me by Leslie Kay, with the briefest possible explanation. Although I was not told this at the time, the idea was to see whether anyone could learn to use the aid effectively without instruction.

It consisted of three main parts: the earpieces and leads; a metal box about six inches by three inches by one inch, containing the batteries, transistors, transducers and circuitry; and a "torch". This was connected to the works by a lead. It was about five inches long, and had an oval-shaped head, about two and a half inches long, an inch wide and an inch deep. Instead of the one "eye" of the usual electric torch, it had two "eyes", about an inch in diameter, which were the transmitting and receiving diaphragms. The whole apparatus weighed about three pounds, the control box being carried in a canvas sling which had been put together by Leslie Kay's daughter. A lead fitted into the base of the torch and was connected to the control box, which carried switches, two for short and long range, and one for on-off and volume. Tiny two-point plugs connected the earpieces with the control box. The control box might tip out of the sling, as for example when one got out of a car while wearing the apparatus; and besides that there were twenty-four separate points and connections where things could go wrong. The apparatus was difficult to disentangle, so finally, after many frustrating experiences, I had a leather case made with three separate pockets for the main parts.

When obstacles were in the beam and it was set at long range, the signals made by the beam were rather like the cries of seagulls. When I went out to try the apparatus, with an earpiece in each ear, leads dangling to connect with the control box, torch in one hand, and stick in the other, I must have looked very odd. The family used to tease me and say: "The man from Mars is going out to commune with the seagulls."

The parallel which had immediately struck me on hearing the first signals from the ultra-sonic torch, as I preferred to call it, was that it was like hearing a new language. If I was to make any progress with it, I had obviously to try to get signals which were simple, and easy to understand. When the family had gone to bed, I sat in my chair in the lounge, and slowly pointed the torch in different directions. The ceiling gave back a fairly high-pitched, clear signal. The signal from the wall about the same distance away was much the same. Without being able to be precise about it, I could tell that the signal from the settee, which was nearer than either wall or ceiling, was different. Certainly, I could tell there was something there.

Encouraged, I stood up, and started to scan around. I was facing the fireplace, and getting a signal from the wall. I moved the beam slowly down, and suddenly got a much clearer signal—clearer in terms of sound. I felt out with my left hand to discover the source of this change in signal, and knocked off the rather attractive small clock, which was a little out of its usual position. This was treatment not calculated to do a delicate instrument any good, and I was not surprised to find that the clock had stopped. Unlike me, my wife had not been immediately impressed with the mysterious magic of electronic progress represented by the ultra-sonic torch, and I felt the incident would reduce its popularity still further—and mine.

However, the excitement of the moment remained. I had no doubt that the signal from the wall was different from that of the clock. If I could detect this difference on first sampling, anything might be possible later on, when I had had a tremendous amount of practice. I thought of all it might mean to a blind child who grew up with the instrument, and learned the language, as it were, from a very early age. I thought of the immense skill which the congenitally blind develop in reading Braille, a skill far beyond that attained by those, like me, adventitiously blinded in adult life. If this applied to Braille, why should it not apply even more to interpreting the world around through the ears? I felt I had learnt enough from my first real essay with the torch—and done enough damage for that matter —and went to bed.

The next day, the moment of unpopularity past, I got the family to help. Andrew was away at school, but during the holidays gave me a lot of assistance with various experiments. In this case I asked Margaret and Catherine to walk silently across the lounge. I stood with the torch pointing ahead of me and indicated the moment of their passage through its beam. This was simplicity itself. The difference was so obvious you couldn't miss it, but what would things be like out of doors, with traffic noises and all sorts of other strains to confuse the issue? It was an interesting speculation, but not one to be put to the test yet awhile.

My instruction, as I say, had been of the barest. It had not even been made clear to me which was long-range, and which was short-range setting, and I was still working on the long range—quite unsuitable, really, for indoor use, but this had not yet dawned on me. I asked Margaret to stand still, found her in the beam, and walked towards her. The volume was switched up, and we could all three hear the signals. As I approached, the signal changed, and sounded very much like a succession of quick kisses. We roared with laughter at this osculatory manifestation.

I went out into the garden, and found I could discern the outline of the fruit trees by the signals in the earpieces. I walked to the end of the lawn, and reckoned I could detect a difference between the signal reflected from the grass, and that from the stone path; but I was unable to detect the step down, which was the first of six leading to the back of the house. This was a serious matter, and I was glad of the caution which had made me retain my stick as well as the torch. It raised a most important issue, which I discussed with Leslie Kay when we were invited to his home a little later.

He took me into his garden, and showed how the signal cut out when you came to the top of a flight of steps down, and also how a series of ascending notes indicated a flight of steps going up. This was impressive, but he agreed that it was only reliable when you knew the steps were there and were looking for them. If you were to walk along scanning the area for obstacles, it was not possible, at the same time, to look for pitfalls—unexpected steps down, or holes left untended and unprotected, with no warning soil at the side you approached by.

"I can build a ground-scanner into my next model," said Leslie. "Then you'll have the protection you want." "That will be splendid," I said, "but until then I don't think one ought to use the torch on its own. I think its present role is that of an obstacle-detector and a supplement to the stick or dog, to tell the blind user more about the area he is in."

For weeks I worked at the torch, trying to learn the language, and find out what it could help the blind to do, and what its limitations were. I discovered that on short-range setting the torch would detect obstacles up to a distance of ten feet. On long-range setting it detected obstacles at over twenty feet. To try to solve the problem of getting adequate information to ensure safety in an unfamiliar area, I went into a district where I had never walked alone before. I adopted a rotating system of scanning with the torch, so that I covered the ground as well as the space ahead of me. My progress was therefore slow, and I felt more restricted than when using my walking stick without any other aid. It was quite a strain concentrating on the various factors—listening to the signals, trying to interpret them, maintaining direction, listening to traffic noises, and trying not to be surprised by the down kerbs which I found it impossible to detect.

After walking for an hour, I had had enough. I was pleased to find a compensating success in the expedition: by using the torch, I detected a bus-stop in a much less conspicuous manner than if I had tried to find it with my stick. I had also discovered that I had to switch off or remove my earpieces when wanting to cross a road with some traffic. It was evident, too, that the torch was no use for detecting approaching traffic.

Although these were disappointments, there were several other compensations. Possessing the torch had stimulated me to venture into areas I had not attempted before. I had avoided the nearest shopping area at times when it was busy, because of the likelihood of walking into people, but the torch gave me good warning of their presence or approach, so that I could avoid them even if they were looking the other way or just mooning along. The signals from shop windows were unmistakable, and much clearer and harder than the mixture of sounds which came back from a hedge. I could understand why a bat will never try to cling to a smooth surface: it must receive the sort of signal which came back from the torch and said as clearly as words: "Nothing to hang on to there."

Leslie Kay told me that he was stimulated to produce his invention when he read of the local blind school, Lickey Grange, getting its own swimming pool. His first idea was that it might help blind children to know where they were in the water. Before joining the staff of Birmingham University, he had been working with the Admiralty on under-water detection; and the study of bats had helped him to develop his ideas. It was an amusing thought to me that the bats' sound system was on the same frequency as the torch's.

Leslie told me that he had often had interference in the signals of the torch, caused by the hooting of owls in the woods near his home in Barnt Green. We only get the occasional owl in the area where I live in Northfield, so I have never had this experience of "hearing" these owl signals outside the range of the human ear.

The torch told me things about my district which I had not appreciated before. I discovered that there was a lamp-post in direct line with the trunk of a tree at one point on my route to the nearest bus-stop. I had been puzzled as to why I had twice walked into this lamp-post when moving away from what had seemed to be an obstacle. It had not occurred to me that there might be two obstacles, each in line with the other, standing like Scylla and Charybdis on each side of my line of travel. I also found I was much more confident when walking alongside a road with really heavy traffic, where the noise of the traffic drowned the noise of my own footsteps, on which I relied so much for information about possible obstacles. It was enlightening to find I could tell the difference, at a distance of several feet, between a person wearing a woollen jersey and one wearing a nylon blouse.

The torch was no use in the rain, when the unprotected diaphragms got wet. I wondered whether it would be any help when it was snowing, or when there was deep snow on the ground.

Although normally the thought of snow gave me no pleasure at all, since it made getting about so much more difficult, I found myself longing for a heavy fall so that I could see whether the torch would be any help or not. Leslie had no idea about this, or indeed whether it would work in the snow.

The first fall came in November. It was not a heavy one, and I was at a meeting at the Bilberry Hill Training Centre—a centre for training boys' club leaders which I had helped to establish—but I left the meeting early so as not to miss the snow. It was a great relief to find that the signals were unaffected. The snow was not deep enough to make navigation difficult but adequate for purposes of testing the signal.

This first fall soon disappeared, and I had to wait patiently for the next, praying that this would be a heavy one. It was, and it stayed on the ground for some weeks.

The first morning after the heavy overnight fall I was not due at the office until mid-day. It seemed just the opportunity I had been wanting. The snow was really thick. Gardens, pavements and road merged into one sound-damping white blanket. If I had been able to arrange the conditions for the test I wanted to make, they could not have been more ideal. They were such that, normally, I would have "conceded defeat" and asked Margaret to escort me to the bus-stop about a quarter of a mile away.

This may not seem very far but there were several possibilities of error. I could stray into fields, one of which contained a deep pool, and another fringed a sunken lane about twelve feet below the level of the surrounding area. No traffic was getting through our road, so this presented neither hazard nor guiding sound. There were trees, hedges, shrubs and houses along the route, which could serve as guide lines if I could get them within the range of the torch.

I donned my climbing boots over two pairs of socks, put a spare pair of shoes for office use into a rucksack, and set out, warmly clothed against the cold, stick in one hand, torch in the other.

In spite of drifted snow, I was able to get a guide line from the features I knew so well along the route: the tree at the corner of the street which was the signal to turn right; the pillar-box at the next corner, which was the signal to turn left; the garden hedges along the next road, and the tree in line with the lamp-post. These were quite distinctive, and normally I would have taken them as a signal to cross the road. I was delighted with my progress, and decided to change my route and make for a bus-stop another quarter of a mile away and nearer the office. I turned left instead of crossing the road, and started down the slope leading to the sunken lane.

The point where I normally crossed this sunken lane had to be pinpointed exactly, because it led to a path between gardens and rough ground dropping suddenly to the level of the road. When there was no snow about, my cue for the crossing point was a concrete drive on the right, leading to the road, or a change from pavement to cinder path if I overshot slightly. The ground on the right of the path dropped steeply to the level of the road, and I had no desire to lose my bearings in this area.

Near the spot where I wished to cross, there were three points which could act as navigational "fixes": a lamp-post just short of the crossing; bushes just beyond it; and across the road, standing like a sentinel at the entrance to the service road, a large oak tree. As I approached the spot where I judged I ought to cross, I switched the torch to long range, and carefully scanned the area on my right. After several attempts I got an unmistakable "click" as the beam of the torch went past the lamp-post. I swung the beam slowly back, and held it on the lamp-post, noting the clarity of the signal with great relief. I turned right, moved forward a few paces, scanned on the left, and found the bushes. As I crossed, I scanned ahead for the oak tree, got a signal, and checked with my stick to make sure there was no error. From this point to the bus-stop was fairly straightforward as there were hedges to detect practically all the way along, which gave an excellent guide-line.

I was jubilant as I approached the bus-stop which I had made my revised objective. I checked the time. Instead of my best time of ten minutes under good conditions, it had taken twenty. I had plenty of time: why not walk the whole way? There was no further possibility of linking with the bus route. The first part of the rest of the two-mile journey had hazards on the left in the form of gardens falling away from the level of the road, but the other side was all right so long as I did not wander off course. It was clear the method worked. I really ought to satisfy myself to the full that the restrictions on my freedom imposed before by heavy snow did not exist any longer.

Continuing my journey, I found myself at one point on the opposite side of the road from where I thought I should be. There were a few other difficult moments, and the whole trek took me eighty minutes, about twice as long as my usual time for walking to the office; but who cared? The torch had made possible what I had thought of as impossible before: yes, it was really a breakthrough. Jubilant, as soon as I arrived in the office, I rang first Margaret, to let her know I was all right, then Leslie Kay. "Guess what, Leslie . . ." —and when I told him the story, he shared my jubilation.

My pride suffered a rude shock that evening. As I walked across the road to get the bus home, I misjudged the pitch of the signal from the torch, and walked into some bushes laden with snow. There was a horrible crackling in the earpieces, but the bus was coming and I had no time to see what the damage was. When I got off the bus at the usual stop, I crossed the road with the help of the conductor, and then reconnected the apparatus: there was still the horrible crackling, but no discernible signal.

This was a bright prospect. Here I was, a quarter of a mile from home, and the snow still as difficult. Traffic had, however, been getting through during the day, and I decided my best course was to walk in the road, keep my ears tightly skinned for traffic, try to follow the ruts and hope that slope and levelling-out of the road would give me my clues when to turn. I managed to struggle home with no worse misadventure than getting a shower of snow down my neck when I walked into high bushes overhanging the pavement from a neighbour's garden; but it was clear there was a lesson to be learned.

Moisture on the diaphragms meant trouble. They would have to be protected if the torch was to be of use in snow, since falling flakes would have the same effect as had my encounter with the bushes. Leslie Kay accordingly devised a grille which covered the two diaphragms, and which fortunately did not interfere in any way with the issuing and returning signal.

Breakdowns of the apparatus had been frequent, so I scarcely needed a reminder not to get into situations with the torch from which it might be difficult to extricate myself if it broke down. Later journeys when this happened served to underline the tremendous value of the torch in conditions of snow. I sustained one or two nasty bumps against obstacles which I had not detected because I was preoccupied with orientation. Once I got hopelessly disoriented when I missed my turning into the home straight, and had to be rescued by a passer-by.

The snow went, and I decided I had gone as far as I wanted with my study of the torch's potentialities, however intriguing; I had too many other pressures on my time. I knew enough to say that I would not be without it in snow. It was eminently useful in exploring a new area, since it could indicate things outside the reach of my stick. When I went into very crowded areas, which was not very often, it helped to relieve strain and avoid embarrassment. I was fascinated in trying to understand its language, gauging the distance away of a reflecting object by the signal's pitch, discerning the subtle differences of signal when reflected from contrasted surfaces. The signal seemed to drop sharply in pitch as you approached the reflecting object. I did not then appreciate that this was really the wrong way round, and that a blind person with sensitive enough hearing is warned by the pitch rising that he is approaching an object.

There were practical difficulties in using the torch for everyday purposes. Hard as I tried, I could not be sure of detecting kerbs, since—with the ordinary up-and-down movement of walking—the slight differences in signal they caused might all have been due to this vertical difference in where the signal came from. Walking progress was much too slow using the torch alone, if you checked against all possible hazards; and you rather needed a third hand for carrying brief-case, stick and torch.

I expected, too, that a further model might quite soon be produced giving different signals, so it would be waste of effort to spend too long mastering the signals of this prototype. With the technique of self-dependent mobility built up over eighteen years, and the knowledge I had gained of the areas I used, I did not want to carry an extra aid which was difficult to assemble, unreliable in operation and calling for much patient perseverance in use. As a result, I used it only occasionally during the next few weeks.

Towards the end of 1962, however, I was asked to demonstrate the torch in a television programme which was going to deal with scientific aids for the relief of physical disabilities. A conference with the script-writer which was held at Birmingham University showed that my mastery of the torch was inadequate for the purposes of the programme, and I started on a crash programme of training, devoting every spare minute to improving my use of it.

The veil of secrecy was now fully lifted. "No publicity like a good story" is an old maxim of the P.R.O.s. Once the news of the torch was released it flashed round the world: "He Sees with Electric Eye", "Blind Man's Radar Beats the Snow", "Sound Machine for Eyes", "Bat System for Blind"—this was the sort of headline which caught the reader's eye in countries throughout the world.

There was considerable to-do in B.B.C. circles over the programme. It was called "A Chance To Live", and dealt principally with powered limbs for thalidomide children, and similar aids. A demonstration was given of the optaphone, the reading machine for the blind which reproduces letters as musical notes. The "bleeps" of the torch provided the programme's opening and finale, and were also made familiar to the world through radio programmes and Pathé News.

The glimpse of the television world was new and intriguing for me. I was amused to find myself occupying the star's dressing-room complete with bathroom, and a "reclining room" with fitted carpets. It was exciting to feel the tension building up through the day of rehearsal before the late-night "shooting". Michael Flanders whizzed around the studio in his invalid chair, taking up position ready to introduce the successive parts of the programme. The producer remained controlled and concentrated as he knitted the various elements together, and the light-hearted relief of all was evident as joyful music closed the filming of the programme.

It was decided to produce fifty torches for evaluation trials by blind organisations throughout the world. Journalists were apt to coin phrases which, though generally accurate, tended by their vividness and picturesqueness to exaggerate the torch's value—and we were all anxious that the blind world should not gain the impression that the torch was the answer to the problems of self-dependent mobility.

During July 1964 I had the torch with me when I took a group of our factory youths on a two weeks' holiday visit to Sitges. The travel agencies had really moved in since my last visit there two years earlier, with promenade and roadside cafés established where none had been before. I was glad of the help of the torch in threading my way round and through these unfamiliar and confusing obstructions, and was again stimulated to move alone in crowded and unfamiliar areas, where I had not before been disposed to venture on my own.

Towards the end of the year I was told that the Council of Information wished to make a film about the torch. Part of it was to be shot in Coventry, where Leslie Kay was now Head of the Department of Electrical Engineering at Lanchester College, and where St. Dunstan's had provided him with a research assistant. The outdoor shots were to be filmed around the area of my home, in Northfield and Bournville. Margaret Thomson, director of Philomel Productions, came over and we worked out the sequences.

On her first visit with the camera team, although they arrived at mid-day, the December daylight was not good enough for filming. On the second and "final" day, which was all their budget would allow, fog held up their arrival until mid-morning. There were intermittent bursts of sunshine, but it was a bitterly cold day. It took the next five hours to get the two or three minutes of film they wanted, mainly because they had to wait for the right sort of light. One could understand why it is cheaper to take a film-set out to a location where the light can be guaranteed, and the tremendous patience needed for making a film out of doors in this country, unless what is wanted is the sombre light of a *Wuthering Heights* setting.

For some time Leslie Kay had been working on a finer method of detecting objects by the reflection of ultra-sonic signals. The principle was that the reflections would come back to both ears as if the sound were emanating from the object itself. He invited me over to his house at Kenilworth to try out the prototype equipment, which was in the form of spectacles, the impulses being registered in the hearing mechanism through pads fitting on the bone behind the ear. I found it very hard to listen to the signals and instead tended to use my natural system of echo location. It was a tiring business and gave me a headache, perhaps due to the weight of the apparatus on my head; I can still imagine it at the top of the back of my head when I recall the experience!

Leslie was disappointed at my lack of enthusiasm, and suggested that I couldn't use the apparatus simply because I failed to understand the scientific principles involved. I was ready to agree they were beyond my understanding, but said the results I got with my ears were equally effective, if not more so. Such miniaturised spectacles may, however, quite possibly be the next line of development, providing blind children of the future with sound pictures of their environment which will do much to compensate for their lack of sight.

In devising their production models of the sonar torch, as they had now decided to call it, Ultra Electronics consulted me periodically about the design of the instrument and of the case it was to be carried in. Their models have come to consist of a torch with built-in battery, and connecting lead and earpiece. It is a sophisticated and convenient instrument, a tremendous advance on the one I struggled with for so long, and much more reliable in operation.

Meanwhile, however, some of the experts were very doubtful about the torch's value. Back in 1962 St. Dunstan's had asked Dr.

Leonard and Dr. Carpenter, members of the Applied Psychology Unit at Cambridge, to carry out tests of the torch at Worcester College, a public school for blind boys. They were just completing these tests when I received my first torch, and had great reserves concerning the device, although admitting it was efficient as an obstacle detector and agreeing that the boys at Worcester College found it useful and wanted to go on using it.

During August that year Dr. Leonard and Dr. Carpenter carried out more tests at Ovingdean, St. Dunstan's Residential Centre in Brighton, with men of varying ages, states of health and intelligence levels who were spending a holiday or convalescing at Ovingdene. The results were almost entirely unfavourable, and it seemed possible that support in this country for further development of the torch might be withdrawn.

I knew Leslie Kay was in touch with organisations in the United States, and feared that the same thing might happen with the torch as had happened with so many British inventions: I could see a product of British brains and skill being developed in America if we were lukewarm about it here. I realised that the torch needed further technical development before it could be of most use to the blind. Until it had a ground-scanner built into it, which would warn of impending changes in ground level, I didn't think the totally blind should use it, except in conjunction with a stick. But I was convinced from the start that this was a line of development which held out real promise for the future, and felt very strongly that it should be pursued in this country. All along the line, therefore, I had pressed St. Dunstan's to give the greatest possible support to the whole torch project. When Dr. Leonard and Dr. Carpenter made their adverse report on the torch as an aid to blind mobility, they argued against "hardware" in general, and recommended better training in the use of the remaining senses and a mobility technique based on natural skills.

I met Dr. Leonard for the first time when Leslie arranged for us to have lunch with him at Birmingham University. His account of mobility training in the United States was certainly impressive: apparently the mobility instructors at the main centres were all graduates, who had taken a master's degree after a post-graduate course in the techniques of mobility instruction.

With such people available, he felt any further development of the sonar torch should be left to organisations over there; and this was an argument I could not accept. I was clear that without any training I had been able to get real help from the torch, even in its existing form, and do things with it which before had seemed impossible. We parted on good terms despite our strong disagreement, but I did not expect our paths to cross again, let alone that we should become closely involved with each other.

Dr. Leonard's assignment to evaluate the sonar torch had made him passionately interested in the problems of blind mobility, so he had obtained funds to tour the United States, visiting the main research and training centres concerned with these problems. In the "hardware" field he found nothing to equal the torch; but he saw at first hand the results achieved by the systematic training of blind people in self-dependent mobility, based on the use of the long cane. Everyone he talked to was full of praise for the long-cane system, and he was tremendously impressed by the posture, ease of movement, self-reliance and travelling ability, of the men who had gone through such training.

I had already tried a form of long cane myself, after hearing a description of the system from John Dupress, who was in charge of a research programme on blind aids at the Massachusetts Institute of Technology. I met him when he visited Coventry, with Alan Clarke of the American Foundation for the Blind, to see Leslie Kay's work on ultra-sonic aids. Despite the loss of an arm and his sight in World War Two, Dupress led a very active life and travelled a good deal, particularly in England. On such journeys he used a long cane known as a "glider".

It was a little over forty inches long, and consisted of a light aluminium shaft, fitted at one end with an aluminium crook and at the other with a round pad of light metal about as big as a penny. The shaft, really a golf-club shaft, was beautifully finished—ridged at intervals for strength and tapering elegantly. I couldn't help comparing it with my rather battered walking-stick, and felt appearances must definitely be in favour of the former. I was not by any means convinced about its use, however: gliding it ahead of you might offer more protection, but would surely make the user look more conspicuous than the natural swing of the walking-stick. Still, I felt I ought to try out a "glider" and asked St. Dunstan's to get me one.

When it arrived, it was certainly very smart, but I didn't like the noise the metal button made as I glided it ahead of me on the pavement. Also, I was always catching the button in railings and hedges, and on the underside of the step as I climbed into buses. George Thornton, a friend and colleague (but no relation) shortened the cane a little for me and fitted a tufnol ferrule, and I reverted to my old method, only using occasionally what I imagined to be the American long-cane technique.

One such occasion was a dark and windy evening when I was returning home from work. As I rounded the bend which leads into the last street before home, a motor-cycle came roaring up. I couldn't hear anything above its noise, but didn't slacken my pace, because I knew where the hazards were—a tree, and a pillar-box; I did take the precaution of sliding my stick ahead of me. It was a big surprise when I caught my left eyebrow on the protruding top of the pillar-box, and felt the blood pouring down my face. The doctor stitched up the gash and it soon healed, but I was left reflecting that there must have been something wrong with my technique.

I didn't think much more about the long cane till after a phone call from Lord Fraser one evening in June 1964. As usual, he came straight to the point: "If we wanted someone to go to the United States to look at methods of improving blind mobility, would Cadbury's be prepared to give you time off?"

"For a purpose like that I'm sure they would."

"We haven't decided anything yet, but it's quite on the cards we may want you to go. I've had a report I'd like you to look at and give me your comments."

The report, sent to the Royal National Institute for the Blind and to St. Dunstan's, was one Alfred Leonard had produced on the long cane training system, urging that it should be adopted in this country.

I was delighted at the idea of crossing the Atlantic; in fact it fitted in almost providentially with our personal plans. Our daughter Catherine had spent a year in Kansas when she was sixteen, as the holder of an American Field Service scholarship. She lived with the Kirchoff family, and went to Shawnee Mission High School with their daughter Nancy and son Criss. Nancy stayed with us during a visit to Europe, and in 1962, when Catherine married Graham Buckley, Nancy was chief bridesmaid. Now Nancy herself was getting married, and she wanted us to attend her wedding.

I told Cadbury's about the possible mission to the United States, and asked if they would grant me six weeks' leave of absence for such a visit. They welcomed the idea, and made it eight weeks, so that I could see something of United States youth work.

Then the months passed, and nothing seemed to be happening about my "mission". At the end of the year, however, the letter of invitation arrived at last, so Margaret and I set about preparing for our visit to the New World.

# CHAPTER 13

## BLIND MOBILITY TRAINING, HINES

This is a book about blindness. I saw a great deal which interested me in American youth work, and of course in the general "way of life" out there; but I shall concentrate here on my impressions as a blind man and on the assignment given me: to undergo a crash programme of training in blind mobility based on the use of the long cane, so that I could report to St. Dunstan's on its possible value for our war-blinded.

For sighted instructors the training was normally a year, and the war-blinded took a course of at least three months; I was to spend a month on the course. My time would be divided between the Veterans' Administration Hospital at Hines (about thirteen miles from Chicago), where the long-cane system has been most highly developed, and at Western Michigan University, Kalamazoo; with a day or two in Washington, D.C., for discussions with Russ Williams, one of the long-cane pioneers.

Margaret read me reports and accounts of the long-cane system. It seemed a tough assignment for someone the wrong side of fifty. In reporting on his visit to Hines, Dr. Leonard referred to a training which reminded him of a wartime Commando unit; he talked of the strain the men underwent being justified by the results. In his book Blindness, which it was part of my preparation to read, the Rev. Thomas Carroll said no course of long-cane training was complete without a course in fencing. I really began to wonder what I was in for, but joined our Fencing Club at the factory and took a few lessons.

It sounded as though I should need a break after such a crash programme. I had long wanted to travel on one of the "Queens", and the five-day voyage would be just the thing to help me get over the strains and stresses of my crowded, strenuous and taxing visit. That settled the return travel arrangements.

For the outward journey, the chance of achieving a boyhood ambition to visit Boston seemed too good to miss. Hines was near Chicago, and Boston was an intermediate stop on the B.O.A.C. service from London. Our farthest point west would be Kansas, since this was the home of the Kirchoffs, the American family with which we were now so closely linked. We couldn't hope to meet all the young Americans we had entertained in our own home since Catherine's year in the United States, but it would be possible to link up again with some of them within the broad framework of Boston–Chicago–Kansas–Washington, D.C.–New York. Besides having business contacts in Boston, Kansas and New York, we were very lucky to have contacts with the Boys' Clubs of America, the American Field Service and the world of blind welfare—all associated with work of an altruistic nature. This gave us an insight into an aspect of American life which the business visitor or tourist does not often see. So our visit turned out to be a kind of friendship progress, strengthening old bonds and forging new ones.

Before we left, the Press had talked of bad tornado damage near the regions we were heading for; but tornadoes seemed remote in the freshness of a sunny April morning as we boarded the Boeing 707 at London Airport. The sighted world's reactions to blindness were reflected in two ways: the slot-machine insurance excluding blind passengers from cover, and the precedence I was given in boarding the plane. This would have done us more good if Margaret had not preferred a seat behind the wing, where we in fact got all the noise of the engines without the better view from the front or the possibly greater safety of the tail!

The flight was smooth and uneventful. Thirty thousand feet up cruising above the Atlantic we lunched on chicken salad with a miniature bottle of champagne, costing only half a crown, to give the right celebration touch. We had been warned to rest as much as possible, for we had risen early, our day would be "extended" by five hours as we flew west to Boston, and by the time we went to bed we should probably find we had been on the go for nearly twenty-four hours. So after lunch I said, "Time for a spot of Spanish P.T.", moved over to the empty row of seats on our right, and stretched out full length to snatch a little sleep.

The value of a short mid-day nap for those who have to work long and hard seems to me out of all proportion to its length. It was not a practice I had consciously adopted, but one which had forced itself on me over the years. At first I had resisted, or tried to resist, the urgent desire to fall asleep which came upon me at various times during the latter part of the day. I hoped this would mean that I should sleep through until the conventional time for getting up. It made no difference to that, and pills didn't seem to help me sleep better at night. But the brief nap helped—I could then go on for hours, facing the day's demands. I believe that a blind person, living the same sort of life as his sighted fellows, probably has to make more effort in order to meet the requirements of every-day living.

My sleep was broken by the sound of running feet. Three children, bored with the inactivity of sitting above the clouds, were chasing each other along the gangway. For them it was as natural and commonplace as chasing each other in the school playground. For me, it was another example of the fantastic developments my generation had experienced. I had with me a pocket tape-recorder, a little larger than a cigar case. On it was a tape with messages for the Kirchoffs from my son, my daughter and her husband. There were also recordings of the baby-noises of month-old Caroline, our granddaughter. I played the tape over to Margaret, and we felt as if we were back at home, with the family and our friends delighting in the sounds of infant contentment.

Boston airport is very near the sea. There was low cloud as we came down for the landing, and the first sight of the sea on our Atlantic crossing was the view of it which made Margaret think we might be touching down in the sea instead of on the runway. However, the landing was perfect, and as we climbed out of the plane, I thought how different the landing must have been sixty years before for an emigrant uncle of mine.

Very few of the passengers landed at Boston, so there was no delay at the Customs. Bob Coughlin, a business friend of one of my

Bournville colleagues, was there to meet us. "I've booked you in at the Sheraton Commander," he said, as he and his chauffeur took our cases and carried them to the waiting car. "I hope you'll like it—it's colonial style."

I thought of the times I had been to Europe, the struggle with crowds, cases and a foreign language. How splendid it was to get this cheerful, friendly reception from someone we had not met before. The postcards Uncle Walter sent during my boyhood had always made me feel an affinity with Boston—and now it was like returning home. But we received the same wholehearted welcome at all the centres we stayed at: in each place new friends were waiting to greet us and smooth our path.

Bob's car took us across the Charles river, past the massive structure of the Massachusetts Institute of Technology and the mellowed buildings of Harvard University, to the hotel. There had been a slight drizzle when we landed, but that had stopped, and there was a fine freshness in the air as we got out of the car. I sniffed appreciatively: a feeling of space and openness. Although I didn't know it at that moment, there were lawns separating the area round the hotel from the built-up parts near Harvard. After we had checked in, Bob drove us round showing us the sights. We had dinner with him, and then returned to our hotel, very ready for bed.

We had a crowded two days at Boston, visiting various cultural and social service places, especially boys' clubs—all very well and lavishly equipped. Unfortunately we had no time to visit either the St. Paul's Rehabilitation Center for the Blind or Perkins College, whose work for the blind has justifiably made them famous throughout the blind world. I made a point, however, of asking people I met, including taxi-drivers and other casual contacts, about how the blind got around the city. The answers given confirmed that the long cane seemed to make them extremely competent—which made me all the more anxious for first-hand experience of a system producing such excellent results.

From Boston we flew to Chicago. Roger Brown, former American Field Service scholar in Germany, who had often visited us during a year spent at Birmingham University, was there with Gus, his father, and his brother to meet us. They drove us out to their beautiful ranch-type home at Wheaton, some twenty miles outside Chicago; a large house in the next field, now a Children's Home, had belonged to Al Capone, who used it periodically as a "country retreat", outside the province of the Chicago police!

We had a wonderful weekend with Gus and Beulah Brown and their children, and then they took us to our first American motel, The Embassy, at Hines. It was a mile away from the Veterans' Administration Hospital, where I was to spend the following week in the Department for the Rehabilitation of the Blind and Partially Sighted.

The title may sound cumbersome, but understandably people do not always appreciate the distinction between the totally blind and those with some degree of sight left. They tend to regard some of the latter as fakes, although many with residual vision have just as serious problems to face as the totally blind. Of the 425,000 "blind" in the United States in 1965, only about a third were totally blind; and the proportion in Britain is about the same. The rest are blind according to one of two definitions: either "20 over 200" (i.e. they can only see at 20 yards what the ordinary sighted person can see at 200), or "where the field of vision subtends an angle of not more than twenty degrees" (i.e. they can't see anything outside that angle). They may thus be able to see perfectly one letter in the telephone book, but not the letters on either side of it.

After seeing us installed in the motel the Browns drove us to the hospital, a big complex of single-storey buildings covering about a square mile. In his office in the Blind Rehabilitation Department Gene Apple, its head, was expecting me. Totally blinded in the Second World War, he had been chosen to fill the post for his remarkable character and abilities, among the latter his skill in self-dependent travel, using the long cane. His calm, controlled manner was matched by his quiet voice, often so quiet you had to strain to hear him. From my first chat with him I could feel we were "kindred spirits".

I already knew a good deal, of course, about the long-cane technique and its origins, but he gave me many further details. I knew that it had been devised by a then sergeant, Dick Hoover, a mobility instructor at the American Army hospital, Valley Forge, in Massachusetts, and that its value had really been established throughout the United States with men blinded in the Korean War. The main idea of the technique is extremely simple; indeed many people have thought of similar systems over the years—one was propounded in a book by one Hank Levy (an Englishman, curiously enough), which appeared as far back as 1852. But the American pioneers have developed a modern instrument and made it the basis of a carefully worked-out system, methodically applied in training and execution to meet most situations with the remaining senses and abilities fully used to promote orientation. The instructors at Hines and Kalamazoo were called "orienteers", at Boston they were "peripatologists".

Gene Apple talked about Russ Williams, his predecessor as head of the Hines department, now doing an executive job with the Veterans' Administration in Washington; and I was introduced to two more of the long-cane pioneers, John Thompson and John Malamazian. The latter produced a cane of aluminium alloy, fitted with a rubber golf-putter grip near the crook, and with a nylon tip. The crook was a two-inch semi-circle, and struck me as incongruous against the length of the cane, which reached from my breast-bone to the ground. It seemed unduly long, and I felt clumsy as I handled it.

Gene then called in Eddie Mees, who was to be my instructor. Cheerful and competent, Eddie was an ex-G.I. who had married an English girl during the war. He was pleased to find I came from an area only a few miles from his wife's old home in Bromsgrove. We went to the small gymnasium, and I received my first lesson in the use of the long cane.

Clearly and simply, without any handling, Eddie explained the grip, and how the cane worked. I was to hold it in front of the middle of my body, with my thumb on top of the rubber grip, forefinger extended down the right side, second finger curled underneath to complete the grip, third and fourth fingers curled in a relaxed position. By moving the wrist from side to side, you could then make the cane touch the ground just outside the line of each shoulder. Before starting to move, you had to establish your line of travel: in this case I stood with my shoulders square against the wall of the gym.

As you walked forward, you made the cane touch the ground ahead of the rear foot, at the spot where the next pace would take that foot; so that you had a full-pace warning of any pitfall or obstacle ahead. The tip of the cane would move from side to side, clearing the ground by about half an inch. It would thus tell you about the ground you were walking over, and you would always be moving into an area already "scanned". The cane touching the ground on each side would coincide with the other heel striking the ground.

I was wearing shoes with steel-tipped heels, a practice acquired during the war, which I had found most useful after being blinded, since the sound of the heels could help produce echoes for guiding and for detecting obstacles. I noted with satisfaction that the loud tap of the cane and the noise made by my heels coincided. For my crossing of the gym, Eddie directed me to a point in line with the door, so that I could check that my line of travel had been absolutely straight. This was something I noted appreciatively during my training: holding the cane in the mid-body position helped me to keep a much straighter course, as though it were like a rudder.

After I had crossed the gym several times, Eddie suggested I should try walking along the shortish departmental corridor, which led to one of the long corridors of the main hospital. I found it easy enough to keep a straight course, so we moved on to the main corridor, which I believe is about half a mile long.

My impressions here were quite different. A medley of sounds came down the long wooden-floored lane, and I felt as if I were about to enter a dark tunnel stretching into the distance. It flashed through my mind that I had had rather the same feeling the first night I ventured along the busy Bristol road near my home, using the sonar torch for the first time in a fairly unknown area, flanked by noisy motor traffic.

This time, however, I was not struggling to interpret a succession of strange sounds, but exercising my senses to the full, and reinforced by the knowledge that I had a buffer in front of me. The smooth corridor floor made it extremely simple to work the cane: I moved forward, and settled into a good pace, feeling that I was doing rather well. My complacency was shattered by Eddie's quiet correction: "You're out of step."

This was a point that would need more concentration than I had realised. I changed step in approved R.A.F. fashion, and carried on. The corridor started to descend, and I became uncertain, automatically slowing up. As it started to rise I felt better, but there were new hazards ahead—patients in wheel-chairs. I moved to the side, caught my cane against the wall, and stopped.

"Just correct your line of travel and carry on," the quiet voice told me. I did so, and we reached an area with more people coming and going.

"Right. Let's go back now. Do you think you can find our corridor?"

"I should get it by the echo," I said. "If I remember rightly, it's the first turning on the left after we go up the slope."

"I'm glad you noticed that," said Eddie. "Changes in slope can be useful aids to orientation."

We came to the corridor, and I stopped.

"O.K. Now just go on ahead a bit, and see what you would have found if you had overshot."

Eddie remarked on the value of knowing the area just beyond and just short of the point you were aiming at, and questioned me about the things I had observed—or failed to observe.

Since I was there to assess the merits of the long-cane system, he had started me off on it immediately, but he pointed out that this was not the usual Hines practice; men who went to Hines normally spent just over four months there. Experience had shown that it was a mistake to allow options in the training, so all went through the same processes, moving to the successive stages of training as they demonstrated their capacity.

Before being given a cane, they did pre-cane training to give them the technique of finding out their position in relation to their surrounding and keeping continually aware of that position. They were shown how to take their direction from the things around them, and to make full use of their senses for gaining all possible information on their environment. They were given practical training in dealing with the situations of their everyday life, how to protect themselves when walking without a cane, how to use an escort, and so on. In the workshop they were taught how to use tools. They learnt to read and write Braille, to type, and to use gadgets like the tape recorder. In the household maintenance shop, they learnt how to fix a tap washer, repair a fuse, and carry out other simple jobs in the home. I liked the idea of an electric iron hanging up so that it could not be knocked on to the floor.

Gene Apple agreed that Margaret should go out the next day to observe a man who had almost finished his training. I was anxious to get her views on the impression such a long-cane user would make on a sighted person. Playing safe, but not really regarding the matter as important, I said: "It will be all right for my wife to take a few photographs, I suppose?"

"I guess not," said Gene. "Not unless you get the man's written consent first."

He produced the appropriate form, which was calculated to protect the men against any sort of photographic exploitation. When I met Margaret at lunch time, she was quite excited. "Do you know what they did?" she said. "We went in a car, turning round several corners so that I hadn't an idea where we were. They then stopped, told the man to get out, and to meet them at the post office." "And did he?" I asked rather sceptically. "Oh yes. I thought he was lost at one point, but he managed it."

"Did they tell him where he was when he got out?"

"No. He seemed to check around for a bit, decide where he was, and then set off."

"Did he ask anybody the way?"

"No. The orienteer told me he isn't allowed to ask anybody anything."

This was very impressive. It was the sort of exercise for a blind man which had not occurred to me, and I went off to find Gene Apple.

"Yeah," said Gene. "That's a drop-off. A guy does it in the area where he's been trained. He might be dropped off in a school playground, an alley, anywhere. He has to rendezvous without seeking any help. It's an orientation exercise."

I was silent. I needed to think about this. Margaret meanwhile was very enthusiastic over what she had seen. "I can't get over it," she said. "These men look completely relaxed. And they're so impressive, because they stand so straight and walk so straight."

"Maybe," I said, "but I feel so clumsy with this long cane. It always seems to get in the way when I'm not using it."

"Did you use a rifle during your service?" Gene asked me.

"Yes."

"Didn't you feel clumsy with that at first, and didn't you get used to it?"

I had to admit that his example was a telling one, but maintained that my cane was too long, and that I would like it shortened. Eddie Mees took me to a spot where the floor was in foot-square tiles. After observing my use of the cane, and the spot where it touched ground in relation to my feet, he agreed that I could have it shortened by an inch. The effect was purely psychological, I suppose, but I felt better using it afterwards.

"What happens when I get into a car?" I asked.

"Get in first, and draw the cane in after you," said Eddie.

"And on a crowded bus?"

"You'll find you learn to cope with it quite easily," he answered; and this proved to be the case. I found, in fact, that my habit of always wearing a jacket, so that I had pockets for the things I wanted to carry, proved helpful in disposing of the cane when I wanted both hands free, for example, when standing and drinking a cup of tea—with saucer. The cane could be slung quite unobtrusively to hang from inside the armhole of my jacket.

However, at this stage I was still not convinced. "What happens when you get into the office, or go to church, or a theatre?"

"You can always dispose of it, like you would your hat, or something. You may also prefer to have more than one cane, to suit your special purpose. We recognise that the cane may sometimes be too long for comfort, but we reckon the advantages far outweigh the disadvantages."

I was much impressed by this frankness—more persuasive than any attempt to argue the point.

During my week at Hines (except for one half-day) I spent every morning and afternoon receiving instruction, each session being a little over an hour: Gene thought this was the most a trainee could take.

I was not allowed outside the corridors of the hospital, but these were long enough and complicated enough to give me ample practice: in developing the physical ability of manipulating the cane, in interpreting the information it conveyed, and in memorising difficult routes. To help me grasp his explanation of a route, my orienteer would draw its outline on the palm of my hand with one finger, taking care not to touch my hand with any of his other fingers. I found my way to the canteen, post office, chapel, bowling alley, and the registrar's office—where you signed out before being discharged from the hospital. John Malamazian explained the progress of the training, and how the symmetrical arrangement of most American towns and cities helped the blind to find their way around even in unknown areas. When a man had shown he could use a cane reasonably well, his training moved to the hospital grounds.

The next stage was work in a quiet residential area, then a more congested one, and finally training in the downtown section. He would be taught how to cope with department stores, railway and bus stations, making journeys using different forms of transport, how to ask for help, and how to accept it, how to deal with help given in the wrong manner—and generally he was turned into a competent traveller. Exercises in the training included finding out information from places like hotels and railway stations, independent crossings at traffic lights and the use of elevators (lifts).

There didn't seem to be much they had missed out.

"What happens in deep snow?" I asked, and for the only time was not satisfied with the reply: this was that snow-clearing in the towns and cities of the United States is done much more effectively and systematically than in Britain, so that blind walkers do not have to cope with deep snow which blots out the usual aids to orientation. I am convinced, however, that long-cane walking in deep snow, using the normal long-cane technique, is not practicable without some other aid such as the sonar torch. I shall have to wait for a snowy winter to put this theory to the test.

Gene had said that his son was disappointed to hear I was not an ex-Spitfire pilot as the boy had supposed. When I pressed Gene to let me try out my long-cane technique in Chicago he laughed and said, "Say, are you sure you weren't a Spitfire pilot?" He did agree, however, to give me a half-day off to observe a man doing his passing out test in downtown Chicago.

I sat in the back of the car with the trainee as we sped along the Eisenhower expressway, over the Chicago River bridge, and through the Post Office building which is such a distinctive sound clue in that area. We approached Michigan Avenue with its whistling policeman, whose whistle controls the traffic in amazing fashion, although I wondered what a stranger might make of it. The trainee was obviously tense and under strain; but then, most of us are when undergoing any formal test—I remember a Braille reading test, well within my normal capacity, which I nearly muffed because I had got test-nerves. The rendezvous point was at the top of the Prudential building, the highest skyscraper in Chicago. This time the man was allowed to ask for or accept assistance. The test went without incident until near its end. He had accepted help to cross at a busy point. He and his escort were nearly mown down by a bus which was in a hurry turning the corner. The trainee agreed afterwards that he had allowed the escort to be on his wrong side.

I listened sometimes to other trainees walking along the corridor, working at improving their technique. One of them, a doctor, had given up his guide-dog because it had walked him down a flight of stairs without warning. As he came along the corridor, Eddie stopped me and said: "Just listen to this guy's touch."

I strained my ears. He was wearing the usual rubber-soled shoes which made practically no noise at all. I could just hear his steps, and the rustle of his clothing, but could hear no sound of the cane.

Eddie assured me he was touching the ground each time he moved his cane from side to side. It seemed to me this was another point in favour of the technique, if you could develop that degree of skill. You could always attract attention if necessary, since the nylon tip was capable of producing a very effective noise; but you could also be quite unobtrusive when you wished.

This was one of the moments which has remained vividly in my memory. Another was when Eddie had warned me I should slow down my stride, measured and deliberate though it was. I failed to heed the warning, thinking the building was all on a level, and that my reactions were quick enough for me to stop suddenly if there were an obstacle. I had not reckoned with a flight of stairs down. Suddenly I found my cane in mid-air, and a firm hand against my chest, stopping me from ignominious descent and possibly accident.

Altogether, although so far unconvinced on the long-cane system, I was tremendously impressed by the men of Hines and the standard set for general achievement. It was equal to the standard achieved in Britain by the best blind travellers I knew or had heard of. It was also stimulating to mix with the quietly competent members of the training staff, and to sense the attitude of self-reliance which they promoted and required. I had had qualms about my visit to Hines, but left with real regret—though to leave the hospital I was quite ready to wait some time for a taxi rather than face the mile's walk back to the motel.

Gus and Beulah Brown who had friends at Kalamazoo, my next training centre, very kindly drove us over there, showing us Chicago on the way and taking in their own university at Lancing—where they and Margaret commented on a blind student using a long cane. It had a red tip, which must have made it rather conspicuous, but the man evidently walked very erect, looking extremely competent.

Except for the Chicago waterfront and the steelworks near Lancing I did not gain any vivid impression of the parts we were driving through; and when we were not talking, I found my mind going back to the whole training system at Hines. Undoubtedly the system produced an impressive degree of self-reliance in everyday life. But although individuals from Hines did extremely well afterwards, I gathered from various discussions that it did not have nearly so good a record of successful employment for its men as the eighty per cent achieved by St. Dunstan's.

Of course the St. Dunstan's training was geared to equipping a man for some occupation, so that he could resume his normal role in society. It kept in constant touch with him throughout his life, and if one job failed was at hand to help with retraining and establishment in another. The average period spent in training at St. Dunstan's was probably about three times as long as at Hines, where the usual period was about eighteen weeks. The Hines staff agreed that this was not really adequate for attaining proficiency in reading and writing Braille, however successful the trainees were in self-dependent mobility.

They also agreed that to raise the Hines percentage of successful employment more individual follow-up was needed. Some of the "orienteers" would have liked to be able to visit men in their home environments to help them sort out any new mobility problems that had cropped up for them. When a man left Hines, details about him were sent to the American equivalent of our local Labour Exchange, the agency responsible for helping him to find suitable employment —or re-employment: a very different arrangement from the individual connection kept up by St. Dunstan's.

As to the long cane, the only times I had used it outside the corridors of Hines were on the balcony of the Embassy Hotel; and then the inadequacy of my technique had made me revert to my own method with a short stick when I thought I was near a flight of steps. I still felt awkward, clumsy and conspicuous using this cane which, although only ten inches longer, seemed so much more.

I tried to compare the early training at Hines with what I had had at Battlefield, Church Stretton, and wondered if the system in the former hotels, the Longmynd and Denehurst, had included any formal training comparable to what Hines was called "pre-cane training": this was really commonsense applied to solving the small everyday problems of not being able to see.

Although it was rather satisfying to work out for yourself the answers to such problems, the embarrassment of early do-it-yourself mistakes could be avoided by quite a substantial pre-cane training, with the experience and ingenuity of many incorporated into a simple system for all. For instance, I had one or two frustrating episodes before I learnt that, when working or doing a household chore, I should have some system of putting down objects so that I could find them easily and without risk of knocking things over; and to use my hand to find a vacant space before putting something down on a crowded surface.

Pre-cane training would also have included various points of "escort technique" (some of which I discussed in the chapter on travelling blind), and how to achieve reasonable protection when walking alone without a cane, for example, by holding the arm across the body rather like a boxer's guard, with the thumb slipped into the belt or top of the waistband to make the position less obtrusive.

Other commonsense points which pre-cane training might cover are trailing the back of the fingers against a wall as the best way of following it and escaping injury; "squaring off" against a fixed object to get a line of direction within a home or work environment; when you have dropped something, pointing your nose in that direction, listening for differences of sound to indicate rolling, or touching significant surfaces like wood, carpet, porcelain or linoleum; avoiding injury when bending down by holding the hand in front of the face or by squatting on the haunches. It was certainly valuable to show men, directly they entered "the blind world", that they were capable of opening doors in a familiar environment or drawing out a chair at table—little courtesies they would still be able to perform for women in that new world. And this was the sort of thing you learnt at Hines in formalised instruction.

Such were some of my thoughts on the drive to the second part of my crash training programme at Western Michigan University, Kalamazoo.

# CHAPTER 14

## BLIND MOBILITY TRAINING, KALAMAZOO

Kalamazoo, which is Indian for "fertile valley", is an expanding town of some 85,000 inhabitants, with paper-making and chemical products its staple industries. The Browns saw us installed at Hoekje Hall (the area had once been a Dutch settlement) in the men's hostel; we were given a visitor's room simply but adequately furnished, with an adjoining bathroom. The students were not yet back, so I had a chance to learn the topography of the Hall and its surroundings without being under general observation. Mrs. Yankee, wife of the tutor warden, suggested one or two places where we might get an evening meal and drove us into town on her way to church.

After our meal we walked back part of the way, exploring the town. Mrs. Yankee was quite relieved when we returned, for there had evidently been a tornado warning over the radio. We gathered there wasn't likely to be much risk in Kalamazoo, particularly indoors, but we decided to buy a cheap transistor set next day to make sure we didn't miss such warnings. According to the Browns, the thing to do if caught in a tornado outdoors was to find a ditch to lie down in, if indoors to take refuge in the south-west corner of the basement!

We went to our room. The central heating system had been functioning to some purpose. We carried out what had by now become our standard practice in the United States of turning off the heating and opening windows and doors in order to get a cooling draught through the room. We could understand why Americans found so many of our houses and hotels cold.

The next morning, Monday, April 26th, we bought our transistor and did a little more exploring of Kalamazoo. Crossing at the traffic lights at the junction of Michigan Avenue and Westnedge Avenue (commonly known as just "Michigan and Westnedge") I noted the rather loud clicking sounds which came from the control box.

"I wonder if I could use these sounds to tell me when to cross," I said.

"I don't think so," said Margaret.

"Just let me listen for a bit," I said, "and you tell me when the lights change."

There was obviously a pattern to the clicks. The important thing was that three clicks in quick succession meant the lights were in my favour, although this did not tell me, of course, how much traffic there was and what it was doing at the time.

In the afternoon we went round to Sangren Hall, which housed the department of mobility training for the blind, and other special education services. We called on Don Blasch, head of the department, who had paid a short visit to Hines while we were there, so we had already met him; in fact he had offered to drive us from Hines to Kalamazoo, only we had arranged to go with the Browns. "See you in the morning at eight-thirty," Don said. "I think I'll put you with Mr. Murphy or Mr. Suterk."

We didn't find the easiest route back to Hoekje Hall, but I felt I could manage the route on my own if I needed to. We went to bed early, both tired out by the travelling we had been doing and all the different experiences.

Next morning Margaret was so sound asleep when I got up at seven that I hadn't the heart to wake her. We had explored the Students' Union the day before. It was in the next block to Hoekje Hall, and I knew I could get breakfast there. This wouldn't be difficult to collect from the cafeteria, since I was trying to reduce my weight and restricting breakfast to orange juice and coffee. The surveys of the past two days paid off, and I duly presented myself at Sangren Hall just before eight-thirty. Cafeteria service, incidentally, is such a common feature of American catering that here, as at Hines, it was sensible that men should become practised in coping with the tray and its contents.

Don Blasch introduced me to my instructor, Stan Suterko, who was also his deputy. They had helped Russ Williams to set up his

original training programme at Hines, before taking up their appoint-
ments at Western Michigan. One of the first things an orienteer has
to do with a new trainee is to establish a *rapport* with him. I don't
suppose Stan Suterko ever accomplished this more successfully than
he did in our first half-hour's chat. The questions asked in his quiet,
controlled voice, were penetrating. His manner showed a complete
respect for his client, without any trace of the condescension or
sense of difference which so many sighted people cannot help
showing the blind. He was obviously dedicated to the system of
training he represented, but tolerant of other ideas and in no sense
doctrinaire. We discussed the pros and cons of the long cane, the
laws concerning motorists and blind people in the different States,
and the supposed advantages of the white stick.

He left me to talk to Miss Crawford, the blind Braille teacher, while
he attended to other duties. She was horrified at my criticism of
American Braille, and of the pundits who had decreed that every
sentence in American Braille should begin with a dot six to indicate
a capital letter. She was not convinced by my pointing out that
capitals did not matter in such a context, and that saving space was
far more important in a system already much too bulky: I had been
put off reading American Braille by this recurring dot six. Gene
Apple had told me that the issue was originally decided by a
sighted person showing his sighted colleagues a transcription in
letter print of what the Braille would look like without the indication
of capitals. Miss Crawford showed me one or two Braille writers I
had not met before including the Perkins machine, which I thought
quite the best I had come across.

Stan returned. "We've got your English habit of taking a coffee
break. How about joining us?"

After coffee, he explained the geography of the department, and
observed my use of the cane along the corridors. "Why don't we
see how you manage outside?" he suggested.

We moved to the road between the university perimeter and the
railway line. There was a grass verge most of the way between the
pavement and the road, but the route was strewn with obstacles in
the shape of traffic signs, telegraph poles, etc. At several points the

pavement was cut by roads and drives leading off. The limitations of my technique were made all too obvious, and my morale was not enhanced on finding that the level crossing, to which I was shown the approach, had no protecting gates. The bell signalling a train's approach apparently did not give a full minute's warning—so I should have to treat level crossings with great circumspection.

Stan had told me I could use the "Gold Room" for lunch: a waitress service for staff was starting that day. To my relief we finished the morning's work early, and I got to the Gold Room to find myself its first customer. After lunch we went out to a quiet residential area with smooth well-laid pavements. The difficulties of the morning were forgotten, my morale was restored. When we got back to Sangren Hall, Lloyd Widerberg, another orienteer, said he would show me a better route to Hoekje, and I gained more confidence as I found I could detect down kerbs in time.

One of the characteristics of the talented orienteer is judgment in giving his client a progressive course of training suitable to his stage of performance. The next morning Stan explained that he wanted to see how I used traffic sound to guide my path. I had never before really used the system of keeping in the centre of the pavement by keeping parallel with the noise of the traffic. The pavement in Michigan was quite narrow in parts, with no protecting grass verge, and as I walked along it with vehicles whizzing past I realised I had better not make any mistake in my line of travel. Stan was satisfied that the lesson had been learned.

"Supposing we go back, and try the route we did yesterday morning."

"I'd like to," I said, feeling I needed to retrieve my honour after the poor showing I had made. The improvement was marked. "Real progress this morning," I said to Margaret, who was waiting outside the Gold Room to join me for lunch.

Over the next few periods, I was introduced to some of the distinctive landmarks of Kalamazoo—such as the fat circular pillars outside the Central Library; the parking rail outside the Y.W.C.A.; the wall surrounding the Kalamazoo Club; the benches on the edge of the park south of Michigan. I learned the symmetrical arrangement of the streets in the downtown area, although their names didn't have the same nice logic. I chaffed Stan: "I suppose you call this street Westnedge because it runs north and south." I learned the one-way system as an aid to orientation. Traffic along Westnedge was one-way, running from north to south. Along Michigan it was two-way, and always busy. I learned, too, to recognise roads which merged into pavements, and the features which indicated a "gas station" (garage selling petrol).

The weather had suddenly improved, and Margaret was enthusiastic over the magnolia tree outside the Baptist chapel on Michigan, which had burst into glorious bloom. I learnt to use the sun as would be difficult (I thought quite wrongly) in an industrial centre like Birmingham with its almost permanent haze. If I knew the time of day and could locate the sun, I could always work my way to Michigan by heading north or south. The traffic flow was unmistakable once you came to this busiest of Kalamazoo's roads.

I was working the cane much more automatically—with much less conscious thought. This meant I could concentrate more on making full use of the echoes and other information which came through to me as I walked along. Apparently one of the locals had been watching me as I avoided a post in my path without touching it at all. "Say, how did he know that post was there?" he demanded of Stan, who as always was following me at a strategic distance, silent in his rubber-soled shoes, ever ready to intervene if necessary.

Stan had demonstrated how I could establish that I was about to cross a street at right angles, and not on a bend—by standing with my toes just projecting over the edge of the kerb, and touching the kerb on my right and left with the extended cane. If the cane came behind me on either side, then I knew I was on a curve, and could take appropriate action. Instead of going round a corner before crossing, which I used to do so as to avoid any risk of wandering into the middle of the road, he stressed the value of using traffic sounds in order to cross straight over without veering. He showed me a lethal traffic sign just outside Hoekje Hall—a sharp-edged metal sheet fastened to a metal upright to reinforce his point about the need to investigate a footpath before stepping up the kerb.

As we left Sangren Hall on the Friday afternoon of our second week in Kalamazoo, Stan said: "What do you say to doing a 'drop-off' this afternoon?"

"Should be very amusing," I replied. "So long as we're back in time for me to catch a plane to Detroit at five."

Unfortunately he was held up for some time at the university workshop, but in due course we set off. He drove around for a while to make sure I should have no idea where I was, then parked. We climbed out, and he said:

"O.K. Now supposing you meet me inside the Central Library."

I stood and thought hard. The Central Library was in Rose Street, the Mall was beyond it on the east side running in a north-south line. Also parallel to Rose Street, but to the west, were first Park Street, with one-way traffic travelling northwards, then Westnedge, carrying southbound traffic.

The first thing to settle was my present position. What had happened to the sun? Was that its warmth on my right cheek, or was I imagining things? Just then it came through with unmistakable warmth.

It was nearly half past three, so the sun should be roughly in the south-west. I checked carefully around me and decided that I was on the south side of a street running east-west. Since we had done very little work north of West Michigan Avenue, it was reasonable to suppose we were south of that traffic artery. There were several possibilities open. Whichever one I chose, I would have to get a move on if we were going to catch that 'plane. I have forgotten now what gave me the clue to head east; but when I came to traffic travelling only southwards, I knew I had made the right choice and was about to cross Westnedge. The area was only vaguely familiar, and there might well be various hazards in my path; but with the knowledge that I was moving into terrain which my cane had already examined, I found I could move at a speed I would not have dared risk in an unknown area using my old technique. Outside the Central Library I checked the squat pillars before entering cautiously. Inside the doors I stood and waited, and in a few seconds came Stan's voice: "Well, you made it."

"Yes," I said. "Do you mind if we get moving. That plane leaves at five, and I have to change."

"That's O.K.," said Stan. "I'll pick you up at half past four and run you out to the airport."

Punctual as always, he was waiting outside Hoekje Hall at four-thirty. We caught our plane to Detroit, with time to spare, and changed to one which flew over Lake Erie to Buffalo. Driving from Buffalo to Niagara Falls, I was surprised at the industrial conurbation we passed through. It also seemed to me rather superfluous that man had tried to improve on Nature by floodlighting the Falls in changing colours. The sound of the roaring mass of water, even though not at its full summer volume because of the slowly melting ice, was still full value for one who relied on his ears for a large part of scenic appreciation. The next day we got our fill of impressions—standing dressed in oilskins beneath the Falls; swinging over the whirlpool in a flimsy, suspended contraption; and descending to the edge of the surging water to throw in lumps of ice.

As the train clattered from Buffalo via Welland and Windsor to Detroit, it took us into and out of Canada for the fifth time in twenty-four hours, and through a tobacco-growing area. In the fields which flanked the railway line there were squat brick buildings such as a child might have designed. They were plum-coloured with imitation green windows, and we gathered that they were used for maturing the tobacco. As the thrill of our visit to Niagara abated, Margaret dozed off, and I began thinking out what I would say in my report on the long-cane system when we got back to England.

It seemed much longer than twenty-four hours ago that I had been moving so confidently through the streets of Kalamazoo, heading for the rendezvous point in the Central Library entrance. Would my short-stick technique, acquired laboriously and painfully over twenty-one years, have enabled me to move so freely in an almost unknown area? The answer was plainly in the negative. With my short stick, I could only move with such freedom in areas which I knew to be clear of hazards. My technique had always had risk as a corollary, not only the risk of personal injury, but the fear that there might be an obstacle which I might not detect by echo, such as a pram with a baby.

The difference the long cane made was that as I walked along I knew what was ahead of me, and could act accordingly. If there were an obstacle, I had a full pace in which to stop. Two days earlier I had done just that when I came to a child's tricycle left in the middle of the footpath, waiting for its owner to come back out of the house. I recalled the two occasions at home when I had walked into the telephone engineers' excavations in Hole Lane. The long cane would have given me warning of such perils. After some thirty hours of concentrated training, the long cane no longer felt awkward and cumbersome, but much more part of me.

Having achieved some skill in its use, so that I did not have to think about my actions, I had also been able to use my ears and other senses to better effect to gather more information from all the clues around me. The protection of the long cane meant a lessening of stress, anxiety, fear; the net result was heightened perception. All along I had agreed that the logic of the system was irrefutable. Margaret was impressed with the upright posture and relaxed, confident bearing of the good long-cane users she had observed. They were thus less conspicuous than the conventional blind man tapping his way along a wall.

There was no doubt about the value of the systematic training in orientation. This was something even the best blind "empiricist" could undergo with benefit. It was curious that in Britain we had not made so much effort to pass on accumulated experience and wisdom in this field. Such training took time; it also took time to become skilful with the long cane. What a boon it would have been to me if I could have had such training during the Church Stretton days! It would have spared me a great deal of injury, stress and embarrassment.

Would men who had established a settled way of life after nearly a generation of blindness want to bother with such training? Perhaps not, but they should be given the opportunity. Getting about alone meant increased strain as one grew older. The protection of the long cane would lessen the strain. Every day there was more traffic about and my walks along West Michigan Avenue had shown that, given the protection of the scanning buffer probe, traffic noises could be used as helpful guides instead of being paralysing deterrents. The long cane would certainly help those who had an additional disability like a hearing defect, and those such as the aged for whom it was specially important to avoid injury. These were some of my thoughts as the train speeded on its way.

Before we caught the Kalamazoo train at Detroit my conclusion had been reached. The system of orientation and mobility training based on the use of the long cane was superior to any other method I had experienced of helping blind people to get about alone. It gave such an assurance of safety that blind people could reasonably be expected to undergo formal training in the system.

"How does the long cane compare with the use of the sonar torch?" I asked myself. The sonar torch had certainly helped to reduce strain in crowded conditions, in areas where traffic noise made things difficult, and where obstacles like prams were to be feared. But its ten-degree beam could only protect you against one hazard at a time; you needed a stick as well if you wished to be protected against an obstacle or a possible pitfall at the same time. Effortless use of the sonar torch with prompt and accurate interpretation of the signals would call for the same amount of practice as that required to master a foreign language. The sonar torch was expensive, needed constant maintenance, and could go wrong at a critical moment; the long cane had none of these disadvantages.

On the other hand, I was not convinced by the answers to my questions about the use of the long cane in deep snow. Under such conditions I would want to have the sonar torch as an additional aid, just as I would continue to find the torch interesting and helpful when I wanted an environmental sensor which could tell me something about things beyond the reach of the long cane, but as near as twenty feet. These were specialised uses; for immediate benefit and everyday use I had no doubt that henceforth my aid to self-dependent mobility would be the long cane.

The experience of the succeeding two weeks confirmed this assessment.

The day after our return from Niagara, Stan said: "Suppose we try crossing at the stop lights today?" I had been doubtful about the value of this item in the training programme. It was useful, I admitted, for a man to know how to cross at traffic lights unaided, just in case he found himself in such a situation with nobody around to help; but I thought it would be a far more dangerous operation in Britain, where traffic was much less disciplined and noisy motor-cycles tended to obscure immediate traffic noises.

We went through the drill. I was taught how to find the right spot to cross at. Usually there was a barrier which acted as an unmistak-able guide, but there was also the noise of the traffic. By noting where it stopped, I could position myself at the crossing. Careful listening would indicate the traffic moving in the different directions and enable me to judge when the lights changed in my favour. That was the moment to cross, decisively and unhesitatingly, having first established the right line of travel.

With Stan in close attendance, and checking my observations, I made two complete circuits at the Westnedge–West Michigan lights, one clockwise, and the other anti-clockwise. We then moved into an area congested with pedestrians so that I could practise shortening the grip on my cane to avoid any risk of tripping people. As we turned into Westnedge on our way back, Stan said: "O.K. Now supposing you head north along Westnedge and cross on the south side of the stop light?"

"Anything you say," I replied, and headed north.

I reached West Michigan Avenue, made my way to the crossing point and checked that I was squarely at right angles to the line of Westnedge. I was just checking the flow of traffic when something completely unexpected happened: a pneumatic drill started up on the opposite side of the road. It was hopeless to listen for the sound of traffic. I expected Stan to come and say, "Forget it, we'll try later"—but he didn't. It seemed as though British honour might be at stake. I was glad I had checked with Margaret on the significance of the clicks in the control box, because I could hear those.

"That's the signal—move, laddie!" I told myself, and stepped off the kerb, feeling rather the way I had done the first time I tried a high dive after being blinded.

I resisted the temptation to scurry like a frightened rabbit into its burrow, and hoped that my stride was deliberate and controlled —in the manner constantly advocated by the orienteers. I stood on the opposite footpath, and waited. At last Stan arrived, as the pneumatic drill continued its deafening cacophony. "I guess that was real mean of me," he said, and we both enjoyed the joke.

In the next two or three days the programme resolved itself into a succession of "drop-offs". One of these had an amusing finish. Stan asked me to find my way to the spot where I had made my memorable first solo traffic-light crossing. I did so, and stood there waiting for him to come up in the usual silent way.

"Well," came his familiar drawl, "where do you reckon you are?"

"South-west corner of Westnedge and West Michigan Avenue," I replied.

"Oh, why?"

I proceeded to detail the reasons, position of sun, time of day, direction of traffic flow, and one or two other points, without realising that a lady passer-by had stopped in her tracks and was "listening in". "My, isn't that something!" she exclaimed as I concluded my catalogue. "I've been living in Kalamazoo these ten years, and I still don't find my way."

I also had an unfortunate encounter, at the junction of two corridors in Sangren Hall, with a girl running to a class she was late for. She was not hurt by my tripping her up, but it taught me that you need both experience and skill to avoid tripping passers-by, including even those who aren't looking where they're going. It made me realise once again that there was a lot more to the long-cane training than I had originally supposed.

Since the training culminated in "drop-offs", there was time for extensions to my programme. I visited ordinary schools where orienteers worked with blind children (who were following the same curriculum as sighted ones). It was good to observe how completely self-dependent they became with the long cane— though there were difficulties I had not foreseen in training them to do things like crossing at traffic lights without assistance. For instance, one angry motorist got out of his car and stormed at us for watching a blind child who wanted to cross the road and not offering to help. Perhaps these children under instruction should have been carrying "L" signs!

On May 12th Stan saw us on to the train for Chicago, and I reckoned I had had about fifty hours' training in orientation techniques and the use of the long cane. The solo trips I had done in Kalamazoo showed me what a sense of freedom it gave for exploring completely unknown areas; and the technique proved its value again during the remainder of our stay in the United States, in Kansas City and Washington. It was fine staying with Henry and Alice Kirchoff in Kansas, and although unfortunately we could not be there for Nancy's wedding, we had the pleasure of meeting her future husband. We had an equally good time with Ken and Eileen Atkinson in Washington, and it was a happy couple who embarked on the Queen Mary at the end of May.

# CHAPTER 15

## BACK TO BRITAIN

On board the Queen Mary I found I no longer felt worried, as I had done on other voyages, about moving around alone in a big ship with steep stairs and impediments in unexpected places. Besides exploring the ship, it was amusing to swim in the shifting water of the swimming pool, or exercise in the mechanised gymnasium before breakfast; to dance on a sloping floor, or join in the other social activities. But I was glad I had a couple of reports to work on; the weather was too cool for lazing on deck.

The conclusions I had come to on the train to Buffalo were crystallised in my report to St. Dunstan's. I supported it with a personal letter to Lord Fraser, proposing that Mr. Suterko be invited to conduct a long-cane training course for St. Dunstaners during the coming university vacation, to give them a chance of assessing its possibilities for our men. My report and recommendations were accepted, and thereafter official St. Dunstan's support for the long cane remained firm. Stan Suterko came in August, and spent a month training six men in its use. I helped with the training, using my holiday for this purpose. It was an interesting experiment and showed that a totally blind mobility instructor can make a contribution, but is not adequate to cover all the aspects of such training, particularly when dealing with motor traffic is involved. All the trainees said they had derived benefit from it, although some doubted whether they would continue to use the long cane.

For one man, however, the training was a tremendous help. He was Joseph Loskar, whom I nicknamed "the magnificent Pole". Totally blind, with a hearing defect, and handless apart from an ability to grip given him by wonderful surgery on his right hand, he had an indomitable spirit. He practised so hard that he raised a blister on his "surgical grip", and had to be rested for a time. He gained new freedom from using the long cane, and could explore new areas with immunity—a facility which proved of great value when he moved with his wife and two young boys to another house.

From his work as a physiotherapist at Maidenhead, Mike Delaney came over at weekends for training. I could only give him about ten hours, but was delighted to learn from him a year or so later that having married and moved to Liverpool, he was finding the long cane invaluable in getting about alone.

My own use of the long cane, from the time of our return to England to the present, has more than fulfilled my expectations during the training period. It took months of steady practice before the physical skill of manipulating the cane became second nature, so that I no longer had to think about whether I was in step, whether the touch of the cane was light and unobtrusive enough, the sweep just clear of the ground, or the cover from shoulder to shoulder complete.

At Hines the cane had seemed so long I felt awkward even carrying it. Now I gradually developed not only skill in handling it, but also adeptness in disposing of it when it was not in use. Beside hanging it from the inside of my jacket armhole, I wanted sometimes to hang it on my arm, as for example when buying something in a shop. I found I couldn't do this with the standard Hines cane, because the semi-circle of the crook was too narrow. So I removed the plastic cap covering the crook's end, replaced it by a nylon button which plugged into the end of the cane, and pulled the crook out into the slightly wider arc: after that the cane could hang on the arm.

As I tried to achieve the lightness of touch with the cane which Eddie Mees had advocated at Hines, I found that the uneven pavements in my home district tended to make me let it fall when it caught on some irregularity. I felt rather foolish searching around for the dropped cane, and also decided it could be a serious matter if I dropped and lost it in an unknown region with dangerous hazards.

One of the canes Stan Suterko had showed me at Western Michigan had a strong leather thong, which slipped over the wrist. This would be a protection against dropping the cane, but could be a source of danger if the tip were to get caught in something moving at high speed, since the user might be pulled after it. An attachment which would break easily would be better. After various trials the best idea seemed a loop of thin unobtrusive covered elastic, tied just above the grip, and slipped over the third finger or the little finger when the cane was being used. It is a simple device which I have found completely effective.

Besides trying to improve my lightness of touch I also practised to develop skill in using the cane with the left hand—a valuable facility when carrying something heavy. Ambidexterity seemed easier to achieve than other skills I had made brief attempts at, like reading Braille, or writing longhand.

On my return to work at Bournville I found the long cane very clearly a protector against the inevitable unexpected encounters with items of equipment workmen had left lying about; and an episode at Brighton brought home to me vividly the cane's value as a "scanner". As I was returning to the hotel along a stretch of promenade which was completely unfamiliar, the tip of the cane was suddenly in thin air. To use the orienteer terminology, I "froze", and then cautiously investigated: immediately in my line of travel was a downward flight of eighteen stone steps.

The scanning technique also helped me to avoid walking into puddles or muddy areas, and even parts of the pavement fouled by dogs. The latter is a point which inconsiderate dog owners might remember when they allow their pet to "do its business" where a blind person has little chance of avoiding it.

The pleasure walking has always given me was increased; now I did not have to concentrate so much, I was encouraged to do the two-mile walk to and from work much more often. Under ideal conditions, as when returning home late at night with few people about and little traffic, I could really step out with practically no risk, and feel the satisfaction of doing the journey in my best time of thirty minutes.

The emphasis on orientation which had been part of my experience at Kalamazoo made me appreciate that my knowledge of the area within a few miles' radius of home was not so accurate or detailed as it might be. I had often thought of getting maps made of Birmingham, but the need had not been pressing, and there never seemed to be time for the task. Margaret's maps of our area had only been designed to clear up points of difficulty.

Andrew was living at home during the months following our return from the U.S.A., when I was extending my knowledge of Northfield and Bournville under the stimulus of the long cane. It seemed that a map which I could read would be valuable. At my suggestion he stuck strips of "dymo" labelling tape on to a map of our area: this tape was material I had come across at Kalamazoo. Wider bands were used for indicating dual carriageway roads. It was a useful map, but the tape tended to come off because it curled up where the road took a turn. Andrew discovered that if the tape were embossed on the Braille hand-frame, it would stick better when it had to bend to follow a curve in the road. It could be cut into strips just wider than the diameter of the Braille dots. The latter could be distinguished easily, and varied so that one pattern indicated a road which followed a bus route, another a road which didn't, and so on. Breaks in the tape would show pedestrian crossings. There wasn't time to go further with the map, but this map did help to clarify my picture of a changing and developing district.

St. Dunstan's, in conjunction with the Royal National Institute for the Blind, had plans, as I knew, to bring over an orienteer from Hines for six months to train long-cane orienteers in this country; yet in the blind world throughout the country there seemed to be a remarkable amount of opposition to the long cane. Correspondence on it in The New Beacon and The St. Dunstan's Review was generally disparaging and ill-informed. Men in key positions concerned with the training of the blind wrote and spoke against it.

I was very disappointed by this, and felt I must do what I could to see that the benefits of the training system were made available to as many blind people as possible. In September 1965 I gave a talk to Midland Teachers of the Blind at Leamington. Miss M. Williams, lecturer in charge of the course for teachers of the blind at Birmingham University, was present and became a keen supporter of the long-cane system. She invited me to speak to her students, and as a result of this and other contacts I found my spare time occupied trying to train three blind people and two sighted instructors in the use of the long cane.

One of these was Arthur Chambers, a physiotherapist St. Dunstaner of the First War, a near neighbour of mine. He had made great use of a guide-dog, but being well advanced in years he did not feel equal to training with another. After a few lessons with the long cane he could get about alone in a limited area without injury—which he had not been able to do using an ordinary walking-stick.

Although some progress was being made, I realised it was merely scratching at the surface. That November I invited Dr. Alfred Leonard, the long-cane advocate with whom I had once disagreed so strongly, to come to Birmingham; he was still on a five-year assignment from the Medical Research Council to study blind mobility. He was enthusiastic about my suggestion that a Blind Mobility Centre should be set up in Birmingham, which would help in the research he was carrying out. It was agreed that the Centre should operate on a trial basis for two years, and should concentrate on non-residential training, a field where there was an obvious need. At first there seemed insuperable difficulties in setting up the centre, but thanks to the invaluable support of two of the Cadbury family, Paul and Brandon, the difficulties were solved. The Viscount Nuffield Auxiliary Fund made a grant of £13,200, and in September 1966 the centre came into being. Western Michigan University generously released Stan Suterko to be in charge of it for the first year.

One of the first "successes" was Mrs. Hilary Greenhill, daughter of a former colleague of mine, who went blind at the age of eighteen. A married woman with a young family, she had not gone anywhere alone since then. Her life was greatly enriched by her new ability to get about alone; she said it gave her a "wonderful freedom" after being "completely tethered" for fourteen years. Unaided, she could visit friends and relations, go shopping or to the hairdresser's, and realising her great ambition—take her children to school herself.

Three months after the Blind Mobility Centre was set up in Birmingham, the Southern Regional Association for the Blind held a conference in Leicester on the subject of mobility. Lee Farmer, the orienteer brought from Hines to train instructors, was present, and there were representatives from St. Dunstan's, the Royal National Institute for the Blind, the Guide Dogs Association, local authorities, teachers of the blind, and the Ministry of Health. Unexpectedly, the conference spent almost all its time talking about the long cane, and successive speakers showed how the tide of opinion had changed in its favour. Clearly a tremendous amount would still have to be done in training both instructors and the blind, but it looked as if the basic idea had triumphed, opening up brighter prospects for a great many people "in this dark world and wide".

Perhaps I was over-optimistic but I am confident that in the long run experience of the new technique will speak for itself, and will finally win the day, and that more and more of those concerned will come to realise that good mobility training, using the means most suited to the individual, produces a new dimension in freedom.

Freedom? Yes, for blindness is a restriction on freedom: its effects have been described as "decreasing the number of options available". In these pages I have tried to show how, for me and others, many of the lost options have in due course been restored, and sometimes to suggest from personal experience how still more of them might be made available. I praise God that despite my loss of sight I have had the chance to lead a full and happy life, and I pray that as many others as possible may be granted the same "cure for blindness" in equal measure.

# INDEX

# INDEX